D0871620

NATURE–
GARDEN OR DESERT?

OTHER BOOKS BY ERIC RUST

Judges, Ruth, I & II Samuel:
  Layman's Bible Commentary
Christian Understanding of History
Nature and Man in Biblical Thought
Salvation History
Towards a Theological Understanding of History
Science and Faith
Evolutionary Philosophies and Contemporary Theology
Positive Religion in a Revolutionary Time

NATURE—
GARDEN OR DESERT?

An Essay in Environmental Theology

by Eric C. Rust

WORD BOOKS, Publisher
Waco, Texas

To Bryan and Karen, my grandchildren
May their generation have more natural wisdom than ours!

PREFACE

This book rounds off, for the time being, the author's preoccupation with the theological understanding of nature and the relation of the Christian faith to the scientific understanding of the cosmos. It completes studies which began with *Nature and Man in Biblical Thought* (London: The Lutterworth Press, 1953) and continued in *Science and Faith: Towards a Theological Understanding of Nature* (New York: Oxford University Press, 1967) and *Evolutionary Philosophies and Contemporary Theology* (Philadelphia: The Westminster Press, 1969). There are frequent references to these books in the present work, although it stands on its own. In particular, the sparsity of footnotes in chapter one is due to the fact that it is a summary of the first few chapters in *Nature and Man in Biblical Thought*, to which reference should be made for a detailed bibliography on biblical material.

The ecological issue has become a major one for our time and has become truly existential; it is a matter of human survival. As Christians we have to question the relevance of this to our own Christian hope and to our contemporary Christian action. It is my contention that these two—hope and action—cannot be separated. What we do now is intimately bound up with our understanding of the future. Furthermore, the eschatological dimension of the Christian faith needs to be given a cosmic aspect. For too long, we have neglected the social and natural facets of our Christian view

of the future. Nature must play its part in the ultimate consummation of the divine purpose. The redemption of nature is bound up
with the redemption of man and of his social order. We cannot sit
down and wait for God to act. We are called to action now because
we live in the tension between what is and what shall be. We are
called to be co-workers and co-creators with God, and our scientific knowledge needs to be harnessed to the ends of his Kingdom.

In the discussion of this theme, I have surveyed the scientific
understanding of the ecological balance of nature and the relation
of ethical responsibility to our scientific pursuits. In addition, I
have surveyed the various secular and theological insights which
contemporary thought has made available. It is in dialogue with
these and the biblical material that the position of the final chapter
has been developed.

Parts of the material in this volume have been used for articles
in *The Baptist Student,* January 1971, and *Home Missions,* March
1971.

In the preparation of this book I am indebted to my friends and
colleagues, Drs. Henlee Barnette, David Mueller, and Marvin Tate,
also to my teaching assistant and graduate student, Mr. Wilbur
Curless. The latter is now busy developing some of the ecological
themes suggested in this book. To Miss Jean Aiken, I express my
gratitude for typing the manuscript and bearing patiently with my
many demands upon her secretarial time and skills. My wife has
encouraged this work as always and ungrudgingly endured a hus-
band who is shut up in his study. The book is dedicated to my two
grandchildren, Bryan Eric and Karen Elaine Smith, with the hope
that their generation may have more divinely guided wisdom in
the shaping of their natural environment.

Eric Rust
Southern Baptist Theological Seminary
Louisville, Kentucky
1970

CONTENTS

PROLOGUE

The gloomy ecological prophets of our time are predicting an environmental disaster which will end life at all levels on our planetary spaceship. Their sole condition for avoiding this is immediate and vigorous action to stem the tide of environmental pollution, control the human population-bomb, and legislate against the prostitution and exploitation of our natural resources. If those who are oriented naturalistically or who are humanists are so concerned, committed Christians ought to be equally so. For their faith is a world-affirming faith, despite an often exaggerated preoccupation with heaven and man's eternal destiny. It is at the eschatological level, however, that our concern for this world ought also to be grounded. For we who believe in the actuality of the Incarnation and who are committed to the promise implied in the Resurrection of Jesus the Christ are concerned with this world in which the Christ became incarnate. We dare to hope for its renewal—a new heaven and a new earth. It is to a consideration of these issues that this book is devoted.

To understand our Christian attitude, we need to clarify our minds about the initial view of nature in the Judaeo-Christian tradition as this is manifested in the testimony of the biblical witnesses to the divine disclosure in Jesus of Nazareth. We shall find in the Hebrew view of nature and the relation of man to nature strange parallels to what science is saying about man and his en-

11

vironment. We must then examine the scientific evidence that is increasingly available about man's evolutionary background in the natural process and about the eco-systems which have been developed within the latter. Man, however, transcends the process out of which he has creatively emerged, and modern science is but one aspect of that transcendence which characterizes personal being.

Another dimension is that of ethical responsibility. We must look, therefore, at how these two are related and especially at the moral aspect of man's relation to his environment and of his use of scientific discovery. Immediately we are launched on the predatory activities of man from the beginning of human history. In Dostoevski's novel, *The Brothers Karamazov,* Father Zosima prays: "O God, bless the animals, they do not soil the earth as we men do." Man has turned what might have been a garden into a desert. What God created with such possibilities that it could be declared "good, very good," has become "cursed for man's sake." Man the predator is no new being, but the crisis has grown to almost overwhelming proportions with the advent of modern science and the accompanying development of technology and history.

The picture becomes a gloomy one unless, in some way, we can point beyond the realm of the phenomenal and see some overarching reality behind the process. After all, scientific prognostications for the future are tied up with the Second Law of Thermodynamics and increasing entropy. The ultimate outcome will be a heat death. If science has the last word, any long term sanction for dealing with our present crisis disappears. At the best, the motivation will be concern for our fellows and our immediate descendants. At the worst, it will be sheer self-preservation and stark fear. But surely there is some stronger sanction for ecological concern than a noble humanism grounded in purely human values or a fear motif with no creative accompaniment. With some deeper ground for our being than man himself, we might weather the storm better, the more so if there is an overruling purpose in the universe on which we can base our hope.

Some indications of new possibilities for natural theology may build a bridge here between the Christian approach and that of secular man. Hence we shall survey various philosophical and theological insights which make some contributions at this point. We must then turn our attention to a possible Christian theology of nature with eschatological dimensions, inquire as to the Christian motivation in ecological concern, and seek briefly to offer some practical suggestions about the Christian dimension of ecotactics.

It may be asked whether the church is not being a busybody at this late day and stepping into a situation which citizen's protest, conjoined to scientific know-how and legislative action, can deal with quite adequately. We must therefore make it clear that the Christian faith does add new and practical dimensions to the situation. This problem of dealing with our environmental crisis is not just a matter of idealistic vision and scientific know-how. The biggest aspect of the problem is in man himself. Ideals, technological skills, and scientific knowledge can all be wrecked on human selfishness, greed, and indifference. This condition has been with us from the beginning of human history, and its roots are moral and spiritual. Sociology cannot get rid of poverty and squalor and racial antagonism without an accompanying transformation of man himself. It is this spiritual dimension which science cannot provide, and it is needed at the ecological level as much as at the sociological. The deep rootage of the demonic in man defies our scientific, political, sociological, and economic efforts to uproot it. If we eliminate it at one point, we find it breaking out elsewhere and taking new forms.

While the world-affirming aspect of Christianity means sociological and ecological concern, the core of its message is the transformation and renewal of man himself. The gospel of redemption has cosmic and social reference, but without the setting free of man to be a real person and to attain in actuality his potentiality to become a son of God, these other aspects lose their dynamic center. Christianity does not offer a blueprint for reformation but the good news of creative renewal. It is not grounded ultimately in human nature but in God. It centers in the Incarnation, in a divine disclosure which is also a divine act of re-creation and redemption. The Resurrection of Jesus Christ promises the resurrection of the whole creation. If the church forgets this essential element of its message, it ceases to be the Church. Man must work now, but God also works. In Whitehead's words, God is our fellow-traveler, but he also is the source of all our spiritual dynamic.

There is also another dimension in the Christian approach to the ecological problem. Nature is created to bear and express the spiritual. We shall emphasize this in the closing chapter. It is one very significant aspect of the Christian sacraments. T. E. Jessop argues that man has to mold the physical "until, under the accumulated efforts of many faithful generations, every part of the material world with which he can have contact shall have been truly understood, preserved in or shaped into lovely forms, and brought into perfect subservience to moral ends." Hence, he speaks of "the vision of a consummation in which this material earth in general, and the living body of each of us in particular, is drenched with the ideal, and through this inner baptism all but loses its materiality."[1] An idealistic kind of vision? But it really is an expression of that hope which Christian eschatology enshrines and which should undergird Christian ecological concern.

ONE

A Biblical Approach
to Nature

CHRISTIAN THEOLOGY HAS TOO OFTEN NEGLECTED the implications of the Christian revelation for the natural environment in which man's earthly existence is set. This is indicated even in the Christian hope where the emphasis has fallen either solely upon the heavenly destiny of the individual or also upon the social relationships within which that destiny is wrought out in history. We have talked about personal redemption and also, especially in these days, about social redemption, but we have little to say about the redemption of the processes of nature. History is moving towards its consummation in Christ and individual souls are progressing to their heavenly destiny, but the cosmos has too often been left on one side.

Now, however, we find ourselves confronted by a crisis in our human existence because of the way we have handled and exploited our natural environment. The issue has become central, and we find ourselves confronted by the question concerning the place nature plays in the divine purpose. Actually, as we shall see immediately, the biblical writers have much to say about this, and it

15

is our human tragedy that we have ignored their theological insights. Ever since science emerged under influences which spring from our Hebrew-Christian understanding of God's world, we have gone our own way and ignored the principles without which there can be no direction for the proper use of our growing scientific knowledge and its technological applications.

THE HEBREW ATTITUDE TOWARD NATURE

We need to begin by understanding how the Hebrew felt about his natural environment, for he did not see it through eyes which, like ours, have been scientifically conditioned. The processes of nature were characterized by two things—their wholeness and their aliveness or responsiveness. The sense of wholeness is a significant aspect of all Hebrew thought. The biblical thinkers saw nature as a series of integral wholes rather than an array of separated parts. At the human level, man was a psychosomatic whole. The Greeks considered the body to be a prison house in which the rational soul was imprisoned, but the Hebrew thought of the body as an integral part of the whole man. For him the soul was both the animating principle of the whole being and a description of that whole. It described the self, the person.

This sense of personal wholeness is seen in the attributing of psychic functions to the physical parts of the body. Man thought and willed with his heart, felt and had compassion in his bowels, and meditated in his kidneys. Again, this idea appears in the emphasis on the resurrection of the personal whole rather than on the Greek idea of the immortality of the soul. Hence Paul's attempt to understand the nature of the resurrection body (1 Cor. 15) and his fear of being found naked, a soul without a body (2 Cor. 5)! Further, our Lord's healing miracles conjoin physical healing with forgiveness of sins. A man's outward condition and inward state are intimately bound together, and salvation has to do with the whole man. At the physical and psychological level man is a part of the natural process, and these are integral to his whole being. This has ecological implications.

This wholeness applies not only to the individual man but also to his social grouping. The family, the tribe, the nation are all viewed as organic wholes so intimately bound together that the whole is affected by the behavior of any member. At the level of sin, Achan's family has to suffer with him, for his wrong behavior covers the whole (Josh. 7:24). This same concept of organic wholeness runs throughout the entire New Testament, but it is seen in a more positive way in Paul's model of the church as the body of Christ (1 Cor. 12). When one member of the church suffers, all members suffer with him. To be in Christ is to be incorporated in his new humanity.

What applies to man applies also to nature. Nature as a totality is regarded as a whole. Within nature there is included a whole hierarchy of wholes such as the various *minim* or "kinds" of living things. In such "kinds," species or genuses, as we should call them today, the individuals comprising them form a totality which continues when they die and are replaced by others. Such wholes have a psychic dimension at all levels as well as a physical one. Thus, nature is viewed as alive, at a far lower level than man, but nonetheless capable of psychic response. So we come to the aliveness or responsiveness of nature.

We see this in the totality of Israel's land, for it is regarded as bound responsively to Israel and as "Beulah" land, married to God (Isa. 62:4). So long as God and his people were not separated by sin, the land was fruitful and responsive, but when Israel went wrong, the land became desolate. Israel was the land of promise, bound up with Israel's hope in the God of the Exodus. The domestic animals also formed a psychic whole and could give a psychic response to man. They had a covenant with man whereas the wild animals had not and could wander free (Job 41:4). This means that nature and its parts have a life of their own which man must respect and not treat lightly. We find in the drama of Job the declaration "If my land has cried out against me, and its furrows have wept together; . . . let thorns grow instead of wheat, and foul weeds instead of barley" (Job 31:38, 40, rsv). The violation of nature means that it will return to the flora of the wilderness. The injunctions to leave the land fallow on the seventh year (Lev. 25:1–7; Exod. 23:10, 11) and to leave a corner of a field unreaped at the gathering of the corn harvest (Lev. 19:9, 10; 23:22) may well indicate the feeling that nature should be periodically set free from human domination and left to follow its own course. Even the sun and moon were pictured psychically as well as physically. The sun pursues its course across the heavens like a bridegroom issuing from his chamber and does so by divine decree (Ps. 19:1–7; Jer. 31:35). How like the birds of the air which know their times and keep their orderly migration (Jer. 8:6, 7)! The morning stars shout together on the morn of creation, and the heavenly hordes can be summoned to praise God (Job 38:7; Ps. 148:3). The stars can even fight against Sisera (Judg. 5:20). This must not be dismissed as mere poetry. The Hebrew saw nature bound together in one whole by a chain of psychic responses.

This suggests that the mechanical structures of cause and effect which have so long been accepted in classical science (but not so much in the new physics!) have no place in the Hebrew approach to nature. One excellent example of this lies in Hosea's description of the way in which the corn, wine, and oil harvests occur. He sees a chain of psychic responses or answers stretching from God through the heavens (rain) to the earth (fertility), to the wine, corn, and oil (food), and so to Jezreel (Hos. 2:21, 22). Each element in the chain has its own life, and a cooperative answer needs to be elicited from it if the chain is to be complete.

THE BIBLICAL UNDERSTANDING OF CREATION

It is in the light of such understanding that we must view the relation of nature to God and to men. To this theological concern we now turn our attention. The Genesis stories of creation, especially that in Genesis 1, make it clear that the creation of the universe is viewed as a historical process, a view very much in keeping with what modern astrophysicists and biologists are telling us. Man came at the end of a long process, according to the priestly story of Genesis 1, and he was preceded by a creative movement that produced the ordered cosmos, the vegetable kingdom, and the living creatures. How like the view of contemporary biology!

Furthermore, God is not seen as a transcendent being remote from the world, but as immanently active and present within his creative process. We see this in two significant emphases in the first story of creation. One is the picture of the divine spirit brooding over the deep, a portrayal of the immanence of the Creator Spirit. The other is the use of the image of the divine speech and the divine word. For the Hebrew, the human word contained the very stuff of the man who uttered it. Once released by the speaker, it went its own objective and detached way. Equally, when received by the hearer, it proceeded to accomplish the intention of the one who uttered it, for example, either a blessing or a curse. The speaker thereby became immanently active in the situation to which he had spoken. When this model is applied to God, the divine speech to the formless void, with which God begins, is indicative of the projection of the divine presence and activity into the developing process of creation. Nor may such ideas be confined to Genesis 1. They recur in the biblical record and find explicit expression in the thought of Paul and the Fourth Gospel. Both Paul and the author of the Fourth Gospel use the model of the divine word to describe the Christ who became flesh and pitched his tent among men. He is the creative principle through whom all things were created as well as the redemptive principle through whose incarnate presence in history there is promise of the ultimate redemption of the cosmos (John 1:1–14; Col. 1:14–17; et al).

Our last references are a reminder that, in biblical thought, the idea of creation is generally bound up with that of redemption. The emphasis is not on the past but upon the future. What began in creation moves to its ultimate consummation when God will be all in all. When God declares the world to be "good, very good" in the creation story, there are two implications in such a declaration. One is that this world is significant for God and has value in itself. He rejoices in what he has made and celebrates his world. Ours is a world-affirming faith which takes the world seriously and believes that it has an important place in the divine purpose. The second implication is that, despite the aberrations caused by natural evil and the sinful waywardness of man, the process of the universe has in it all the potentialities to accomplish God's purpose. Man may become alienated from God and his fellows, and he may mar the movements of nature, but God has made a world which contains all the possibilities for ultimately fulfilling his plan. In this light also it is good. But we note that even here it is the end and not the beginning that gives significance to the creative process. Eschatology takes precedence over creation.

In the Old Testament there is a stream which emphasizes the first implication noted above and which is especially enshrined in the Wisdom Literature. In common with the wisdom of similar circles found throughout the ancient Near East, the wise men of Israel were primarily concerned with a certain practical shrewdness, an attitude to life grounded in human experience. Concerned with wisdom garnered from the business of everyday living, they affirmed human life and celebrated their world. Undoubtedly much of the material gathered in postexilic literature like the Book of Proverbs goes back to early days. Such an attitude would seem to point to days when Hebrew life was in a period of affluence, and it is significant that Solomon is traditionally identified as the archetype of wisdom. Yet Israel's faith in God had to be expressed in the growing accumulation of wise sayings and practical advice. Hence the distinctive mark of the Hebrew stance is to see wisdom as God's gift rather than as a mere accumulation of worldly common sense. As such, we can understand how the divine Wisdom becomes central in the growing movement of Wisdom thought.

Wisdom is pictured as a personified divine attribute, a reality which is divine and yet, in some sense, stands apart from God as well as being in God. We see this in Proverbs 8:22–30, where Wisdom is seen as God's agent in creation, brought forth before that creation began (vv. 22–26), present when God created the heavens, the earth, and the sea, standing by his side as his master workman, and daily his delight (vv. 27–30). God is immanent in creating, and Wisdom shares in his creative activity. In Job, too, we have a noble poem which celebrates the place of the divine Wisdom in the created order (Job 28). Again, it is pictured poetically as apart from the Creator, with its own abiding place and its own path (Job 28:23). God saw it when he established the statutes or decrees for the rain and the way of the lightning (Job 28:26). It is reflected in all of God's works. In the postcanonical books Ecclesiasticus, chapter 24, and the Book of Wisdom, chapters 7 and 9, the same idea is echoed. Wisdom has moved now to the position of a complete hypostasis within the divine being. God alone knows and possesses Wisdom. He pours her forth upon all his works so that she covers his works like a mist (Ecclus. 24:3). She dwells in the heights with God, but walks the watery deeps, ruling the seas, the earth, and all peoples, and finding a special dwelling place in Israel (Ecclus. 24:4–8). This divine Wisdom transcends all human understanding, and for man the lesser wisdom of fearing God is preserved (Ecclus. 24:28, 29; 23:27; 25:11; cf. Prov. 9:10). The Book of Wisdom celebrates still more thoroughly the immanence of wisdom in all created things, as the breath of God's pervading power, penetrating all things as their artificer, and imparting to men the secrets of nature (Wisd. 7:24–26; 7:17–22).

Zimmerli indicates a doctrine of creation associated with the wisdom tradition. He finds this to be equally as early as but more humanistic than the same doctrine in the Genesis stories, associated with the "salvation history" and covenant tradition. The wise men were in active dialogue with their world and rejoiced in it. They celebrated its wonders. Their influence may indeed be seen in some of the great nature psalms. Psalm 136 declares that by wisdom God made the heavens (v. 5). Psalm 104 celebrates God's works, all of them made in wisdom (v. 24). Psalm 24 declares the earth to be his, and Psalm 8 rejoices in his creative activity. The creative wisdom towers above man's intellect and penetrates his innermost thoughts (Ps. 139:1–4). Indeed, the whole creation is called upon to celebrate its Creator (Ps. 148).

It was not so much man's sin but the glory of life that occupied the center of the stage for the wise men. Life was good, something to be enjoyed, and the world was the setting for such a rich human existence. The ethical precepts of the wise were offered as means of making such an existence possible. Von Rad sees the age of Solomon with its success and affluence as a crucial period in Israel's faith, a kind of secularization when a this-worldly attitude began to develop and a type of gentlemanly life began to emerge.[1] This may well have been the time when wisdom began to flourish and with it a new understanding of and rejoicing in creation. If so, the tradition about Solomon's wisdom is not without some foundation. Nature existed by its own right. It could be celebrated for its manifestation of the divine Wisdom. Thus the tremendous passages in Job 38:1–38 and Job 38:39–39:30 offer a brilliant description of natural phenomena and a review of the whole animal world and then conclude with an utterance, the burden of which is, "This is the world that I have made, could you make it and run it. Yet you dare to criticize me." If God does all this, how can men dare to criticize his administration of the universe? Another speech follows until Job declares, "Thou canst do all things" (Job 42:1). The world was good, as the human life in its setting was good. This is a warning that a radical redemption theology grounded in biblical thought needs to be compensated for by a more humanistic creation theology. Does the world play a part in God's purpose apart from man? Is this creation theology a point of contact with secular man?

The second implication referred to above brings into focus the redemptive aspect. This is elaborated in New Testament thought and made central, although the idea of the divine Wisdom as well as that of the divine Word undoubtedly influenced the use of the theme of the cosmic Christ by Paul and the writer of the Fourth Gospel.

The Christian faith expressed in the New Testament affirms that the end of history, its ultimate consummation, has become present in the midst of history in Jesus of Nazareth. In his life, death, and resurrection we have the "incarnate eschaton," the Christ in whom all things will be summed up, present already in the process and directing it towards its goal, despite the alienation of his creatures. Hence, we have a movement of thought not from creation to redemption but from redemption to creation. The central vision is fixed on the redemptive acts in history and their ultimate consummation. Consequently, in the Old Testament, the prophet of the Exile moves from the redemption of the exiles in Babylon to the process of creation in which the world was formed and the creation of the nation at the crossing of the Red Sea. As he sees the wilderness being transformed for the return of the exiles, his mind moves back to the creative transformation of the formless void and the creative formation of a nation out of a loose confederation of tribes. The struggle of God with the primordial formless void and the Exodus provide models for the exilic redemption, but it is the redemption that triggers concern for the original creative act. He who can transform nature for his returning people must be the One who made nature. Here is the implicit logic. The same thought is echoed in the New Testament. The redemption in Christ provides the setting for the Pauline and Johannine understanding of creation already discussed. The promise of an ultimate consummation present in the incarnation of the Christ points back to what was already potent in the initial creative act. The new creation in Christ points back to the old creation at the beginning. The resurrection of the Lord promises an ultimate resurrection of all things in which the original creation will find fulfillment.

MAN'S RELATION TO NATURE

It is within such a setting of hope and promise that we must understand the biblical stance on man and man's relation to nature. In the creation story of Genesis 1, the picture of man as in God's image is given three dimensions—his relation to God, his relation to his fellows, and his relation to nature (Gen. 1:26–31). He is created to live in responsive relationship with God, to be addressable by God and obedient to God's will, to walk with God as the story of Genesis 2 pictures it symbolically in its garden setting. He is also to live in responsible relationship with woman, a type for all human relationships since the male/female relation is the most intimate of these. He is a social and ethical creature. Finally, he is given dominion over the earth and the lower creation to subdue it. Here again ethical responsibility is implied. For such subjection of the earth is always under that God in whose image man is made and in whose purpose man must play his part. Along with the injunction to subdue the earth there is the instruction to multiply by procreation. Wise procreation under God would have its needs met by an ordered environment controlled in the interests of the divine purpose.

We must remember that man is not completely cut off from the animal order. He is "soul," and the word means both the animating principle in man and also his personal totality, his self, in all its aspects. The biblical description of "soul" is quite different from the Greek idea. The body is no prison house of a soul but a part of that personal psychosomatic whole which the word "soul" designates. The soul both animates and includes the body. Yet, though man is distinguished from the animals because he is made in the divine image, he is also one with them so that he and they are all flesh. "Flesh" is something that man shares with the animal creation. "All flesh" can describe both (Gen. 7:4, 23). "Flesh" is the common stuff of the human race and all created things. It is the dead stuff out of which man is individualized, and the animating presence of the soul turns it into a living whole (Job 34:14, 15; Ezek. 37:8–10). The human personal wholeness, the soul, is what distinguishes man from the animals which are, at their own level, psychic and responsive wholes. All are creaturely flesh in contrast with God, who is "spirit."

Paul uses the same idea and develops it in a new direction in relation to his understanding of sin. He speaks of man living in the flesh, in the sphere of human existence (Phil. 1:22; Gal. 2:20). He even differentiates between the flesh of beasts, birds, and fishes and that of man (1 Cor. 15:39). Man walks in the flesh (2 Cor. 10:3). The flesh is often identified with the outward and visible (2 Cor. 11:18, cf. 2 Cor. 5:12; also Rom. 2:28, 29). The flesh is weak and perishable, but Paul makes it bear ethical characteristics not mentioned in the Old Testament. Here the flesh that characterizes man becomes distinctive from the flesh that characterizes the animals. Their spheres of earthly existence stand apart, for man is tempted to trust in the flesh, to have the mind of the flesh, to set his eyes on the things seen and outward, and to ignore the invisible, spiritual, and transcendent (Rom. 8:8, 9; 2 Cor. 1:17; 1 Cor. 1:26). As such, the flesh becomes the seat of sin, but there is no advocacy of a dualism. The human flesh is not evil in itself. It is weak and creaturely. Here sin and the demonic powers find their lodgment in and entrance into man's personal whole. With his eyes on his world, man is tempted to exploit it and use it for his own ends. His flesh, his earthly sphere of existence, and his creaturely "stuff," open him up to creaturely rebellion and arrogance.

The characteristic model for man's relationships is that of covenant. In such a relationship the dominant motif is that of loyal or steadfast love. The partners are pledged to keep faith, to manifest loyalty and faithfulness to one another. Where one partner is the superior, as in the divine/human relationship, the greater offers the conditions; the lesser pledges himself to loyal obedience, and the greater pledges to be steadfastly loyal to his partner. Thus God requires obedience of man but also declares his steadfast love. Within this setting, the biblical writers see a structure of covenants between God and man, between man and man, between God and nature, and between man and nature. Such a structure emphasizes the personal nature of God; it preserves the freedom of man as a person; it safeguards the quasi-independence of nature at all levels so that all things have a life of their own; and it rules out any suggestion of a naturalistic pantheism. God is a transcendent presence, other than his creatures, even though immanently active and creatively present in their lives.

The covenant relationship of God to man has been emphasized in biblical studies almost ad nauseam. All of us are familiar with the Sinai covenant. We have learned to differentiate between the wilderness tradition of Sinai, with its divinely given conditions framed in the demands of the Decalogue, and the Abrahamic covenant with its unconditional promise. In the latter we have seen the extension in the Davidic covenant with its "sure blessings." We have moved from Jeremiah's promise of a new covenant to its fulfillment in our Lord and his Church, the people of the new covenant. But often we have forgotten that behind this there is a primary covenant of the Creator with men made in his image, often called the Adamic or the Noachic covenant. It is expressed in Genesis 1:28–30, discussed above, and in the Noah story where God promises to preserve the regularity of nature despite the waywardness of man (Gen. 9:8–17).

This latter covenant is of significance for our discussion for it involves not only all men but the whole creation. There is implied a covenant of God with nature which also involves man. The implications so far as nature is concerned are seen in the frequent biblical references to nature's dependence upon its Creator. He blesses the field by sending the rain upon it (Gen. 27:27, 28) and makes the grass grow upon the mountains (Ps. 147:8). The food of beasts and birds is his gift (Ps. 147:9), and the young lions seek their meat from him (Ps. 104:21). He controls the stormy wind and the mounting waves upon the sea (Ps. 107:25), while the lightnings are his handiwork and winds come forth from his treasure chambers (Jer. 10:13). The continuance of the animal order is referred to as God's creating, just as death comes when he takes away their breath (Ps. 104:29, 30).

There is a sense both of God's immediate and immanent activity in nature and of nature's quasi-independence. On the one hand, all nature is under his immediate control and directly dependent on him. It is directly linked to his activity, and its conservation is regarded as a continuation of his creative work. Indeed, the verb "to create" can be used of his acts in course of the created order as well as its organization (Isa. 40). On the other hand, God grants to nature and its hierarchy of wholes their own life while he conserves them. They have their own regularities and capacities for psychic response. This is specifically expressed in the concept of their decrees or statutes. Through such decrees his conserving activity finds expression. They are energies wholly dependent on his support. Such statutes do not limit his activity as so often was implied in the idea of scientific law in the old days of classical physics. They represent inherent energies which God has granted to natural wholes and which he preserves. The fruit comes from the inherent energies of the tree, just as the corn develops from the seed (Ezek. 34:27). God prepares the corn which covers the valleys after the rain has fulfilled its function (Ps. 65:9). But the rain, too, is God's gift (Isa. 55:10; Ps. 65:9–13), while man must also play his part. He must cooperate by preparing the soil, and the knowledge of the long and patient processes involved in this is also the gift of God (Isa. 28:24–29).

At once we are brought face to face with man's covenant with nature. God's activity underlies the inherent energies of nature, the natural processes, and also the human agencies which contribute to the development, but man must cooperate. On God's side his statutes in the natural order will stand firm. This is part of the assurance that he will not break his covenant with his people (Jer. 33:25, 26). Yet man is also responsible under God. The domestic animals belong to man and are a part of his psychic totality. But man must respect their life (Prov. 12:10). He must rest them on the Sabbath (Exod. 20:10; 23:12). Indeed, he has a covenant with them by which they have become his servants (Job 41:4). The covenant involves him also in responsibilities, and these he must respect. With the wild animals, however, he has no covenant. They are only in God's covenant of which the rainbow is the sign (Gen. 9:16). Hence they are free to go their own way in God's world. The human covenant with nature is reflected also in the passages already cited which indicate respect for the land and its harvests.

We need to remember that the more humanistic and possible lay creation theology of the wisdom tradition emphasizes man's place in the natural order. It regards him as God's vicegerent, a kind of king over nature in his divinely given right. In modern jargon, it celebrates man's maturity. Psalm 8 reflects this tradition when it speaks of man as having, by divine assignment, all things under his feet and being given dominion over God's creation (vv. 5–9). The Genesis 1 story in the priestly tradition of Jerusalem runs, in many places, parallel to that of the wise men, but diverges in a bigger concern with man's sin. What is clear is that the view of sin in man and perversion in nature to which we now turn our attention needs to be tempered by a more humanistic strain. Despite all that the Bible says about sin and the need for redemption, man is not so radically lost that his Creator does not continue to trust him with the stewardship of his world!

Even the wise men with their humanistic stance were increasingly aware of the inequities of human existence. The man who lived by the moral precepts of the wise did not necessarily thrive materially. The prosperity of the wicked was a very real issue for the wise, and it was evident that prudential ethics was not the whole answer. The drama of Job reaches sublime heights as the author wrestles with this demonic aspect of human existence, and finally he has to leave it in the recognition of the divine mystery. Thus humanism, even religiously inspired, does not have the answer. Even the wise man cries out for an ultimate divine redemptive activity. Job has to hope that God will put things right beyond death and to declare that God is his redeemer, his kinsman-vindicator. So we turn to the issue of the sin of man and the perversion of nature.

THE MISDIRECTION OF NATURE

God is seen as creating man to live in a garden with perfect understanding and empathy toward his environment and in respon-

sible and loving relationship with his fellows. The stories of Genesis
2 and 3 point to this, but Genesis 3 indicates that there is a "crisis
in Eden." Man, created to live in a garden, finds himself in a
wilderness. The symbolism of Genesis 3 is significant. In breaking
his covenant with God, man breaks his covenant with his fellows
and with nature. Instead of walking humbly with God, peaceably
with his fellows, and as a steward of his natural environment, he
takes the road of arrogance, selfishness, and greed. However we may
analyze the profound insights into the roots of human sin in the
story of the Garden, it stands clear that man's alienation from God
springs out of creaturely pride and insecurity commingled. Possessing the divine gift to subdue the earth, he seeks the way of arrogant
over-lordship and greedy exploitation. His alienation from God
brings alienation from nature. The chaos from which God called
him and all living things begins to return. The garden gives place
to the wilderness, and the covenant with nature is broken. Instead
of subduing nature for God's ultimate purpose, man exploits it for
his own ends. But nature is responsive, and it hits back at man. By
their sin men have lost their true relationship to the natural order,
and the natural order itself becomes perverted. The flora of the
garden gives place to the flora of the wilderness. The thorn and the
thistle take up their abode and threaten man's source of sustenance
(Gen. 3:18), while the ground itself is cursed (Gen. 3:17). The
idyllic possibilities in the divine intention have been lost, and man
wanders as an alien in his world because he is alienated from his
Creator.

In the Genesis narrative, the relation of the animals to man has
to be reconstructed after the Flood. Men, by their sin, have lost the
true relationship of peace and harmony with the natural order. God
has promised in his covenant not to allow the primordial chaos to
take over any more as it did in the Flood. But the pattern of relationship is different. The animals are to be related to man by fear,
not trust (Gen. 9:2, 3). God may make his covenant and set his
bow in the heavens as a sign, but man's sinful state will have its
repercussions upon the natural order. This vision recurs often. The
fruitful land becomes a salt desert because of the wickedness of its
inhabitants (Ps. 107:33, 34). Moab and Ammon became a wilder-

ness of nettles and salt pits, a perpetual desolation, because of their treatment of God's people (Zeph. 2:9). Because of its peoples' sin, Edom's pasture will be made desolate (Jer. 49:20), and Hazor will become a dwelling place of jackals, a desolation forever, in which no man can dwell (Jer. 49:33). Even the wild animals, roving at will, are a sign of man's weakness, and God uses their existence to reduce Job to silence and to an overwhelming sense of creatureliness (Job 38:39; 39:26).

In New Testament thought, the sin of man and the crisis in the natural order are bound together. Paul declares that the creation has been made subject to emptiness, not by its own choice but by reason of him who subjected it (Rom. 8:20). Contemporary exegesis usually interprets "creation" as meaning the whole created order, not just man. It further identifies "him who subjected it" with God. The passage may indeed reflect the Genesis story and refer to the divine judgment after the Fall, when the ground is cursed for man's sin. Yet this corruption of nature has in it a dimension of hope. The creation as well as man is looking to the day when it shall be freed from the bondage of corruption and share in the glorious liberty of the children of God. Bultmann cogently suggests that the creation "has a history which it shares with man."[2] As Paul sees it, the whole process of nature seems subject to emptiness, futility. In the animal order and in the realm of plants, the circle of birth and death repeats itself, continuing ever onwards in an unending stream of descendants. From the naturalistic point of view it seems just a case of reproduction succeeding reproduction, with the blind struggle for existence thrown in. Futility, dissolution, decay abound. We may ask with reason whether all natural evil is to be accounted for on the basis of human sin, but evil in man and evil in nature are still bound together. Man is organic to the natural process. He cannot be completely separated from his context in the created order, even though he is in the divine image. The surd quantity in nature interacts with man's misuse of his freedom, and the latter leads to a misdirection of nature in which the travail of the natural order is intensified.

Paul attempts to deal with the surd quantity in nature itself by his concern with the demonic forces which hold the world in the thrall. Hence his concept of "the flesh."

THE "INCARNATE ESCHATON"

We thus face a situation in which not only man but his natural environment stand in need of redemption. This is what is implied in the Incarnation. Our Lord's ministry reflects a concern with both human sin and natural evils like disease. He was concerned to save men in their psychosomatic wholeness, to make them real persons in the full sense of the word. Hence, forgiveness of sins and bodily and mental healing become concomitant in many of his deeds. He celebrated the harmony and peace of nature in contrast to the pride and greed of man. The lilies have a glory of their own which is God's gift, whereas Solomon, free to choose his raiment, may cease to express the divine glory which is manifested in the flowers (Matt. 6:28, 29).

As New Testament men sought to express the significance of our Lord's life, death, and resurrection, even though their primary emphasis fell upon the recreation of man, they did not leave out man's creaturely setting. Redemption, the setting free of man from all inhibiting powers, involved nature also. In the ultimate consummation, already promised in the resurrection of Jesus, the whole creation would be involved. The significant point is that the Word took flesh, that the Son of Man took the form of a servant. We see God identifying himself with his creatures and drawing their life into his own. Moreover the Resurrection is seen as the harbinger of hope, the promise of a new age. The new creation in Christ means a new humanity in a new order. This is reflected in the understanding of the cosmic Christ, the Word who takes flesh, as noted above. Jesus the Christ is the incarnate presence in history of him in whom all things were created and in whom we exist (1 Cor. 8:6). His presence in history carries the original creation to a new level in the promise of a new creation in which the alienation of man and the perversion of the natural order shall ultimately be removed.

The New Testament writers do not, however, leave all to a future consummation. The believer has, in the presence of the Spirit, an earnest of his future inheritance (Rom. 8:23). Men need not be enslaved to the power of sin and the other demonic forces that plague their existence. They are adopted as sons in God's family and are placed in a relation to God in which they no longer need be afraid. They are joint heirs with Christ (Rom. 8:12–17; Gal. 4:6, 7). They may already enjoy the life of the coming age (John 6:39, 40).

This preoccupation with human recreation here and now should not, however, hinder us from a more humanistic attitude towards this world. The characteristic stance of the New Testament does not completely shut out some present concern with the natural order. The author of Hebrews cites Psalm 8 and declares that though we do not see all things put under man, we see Jesus. Is he implying that in Christ some reconciliation with the natural order is presently possible? Paul declares that already all things belong to the saints since they are Christ's and Christ is God's (1 Cor. 3:21–23). To the first man, Adam, was given the reign over the world as God's vicegerent. Now in the second man, the Christ, men succeed where hitherto they have failed. They are free under God to rule the world. The Kingdom is theirs now, and it is manifest in the quality of life which they possess. It is significant that natural science was brought to birth within the Christian tradition and that its original humanistic accompaniment in the Renaissance had Christian roots. Are science and the secular stance of our day completely out of step with the Christian affirmation of a new creation and a new humanity in Christ?

THE ULTIMATE CONSUMMATION

Thus the ultimate consummation is viewed in cosmic dimensions. The whole universe, nature as well as man, is moving towards the final accomplishment of the divine purpose. In the Old Testament the prophets see a transformed nature sharing in the ultimate restoration of God's people. Nature and man will be at peace together as man is reconciled to God and to his fellows. God will create out of the chaos consequent upon his judgment a new heaven and a new earth more glorious than anything that has gone before (Isa. 65:17; 66:22). In that new world, the wild animals will be at peace with man and consort without contention with the domestic animals (Isa. 11:6–9; Hos. 2:18). A healing stream, flowing from the altar of sacrifice, will bring fertility to the land, cleanse the salt from the waters of the Dead Sea, and allow fish to live in its waters (Ezek. 47:1–12). The Mount of Olives will split asunder, and Jerusalem will dominate the landscape as the mountain structures around it are changed (Zech. 14:4).

As in the Old Testament, so in the New. The redemption centers in sinful man, but all creation will share in it. Paul sees the whole creation groaning and travailing in pain together, waiting for the unveiling of the sons of God (Rom. 8:19). It is straining forward expectantly, looking for the ultimate redemption. Again, the apostle sees "all things" being reconciled to God by the sacrifice of Christ, and "all things" being summed up in Christ (Col. 1:20; Eph. 1:10). In both cases "all things" is made to include things in heaven and things on earth. Finally, the Seer of the Apocalypse looks for a new heaven and a new earth, as the new order comes to birth (Rev. 21:1). The heavens will be rolled up like a scroll, and the mountains and islands will be displaced (Rev. 6:14), so that the whole creation may put on a new dress.

The Implications of Biblical Thought

The foregoing analysis of the biblical approach to nature carries with it certain implications.

For one thing it regards nature as something which is to be celebrated in and for itself, something in which the Creator rejoices and which forms an intimate part of his purpose. He declares it to be good, for it contains all the potentialities for fulfilling its part in his plan.

In the second place, man in his bodily form is a part of nature even though he stands above it. God has given man the capacity to subdue it and direct its processes for God's glory. Hence, man is bound to nature in a responsive and responsible relationship, even as he is bound to God. His scientific ability is a divine gift, and his scientific methodology is rooted in the Judaeo-Christian tradition.

In the third place, man in becoming alienated from God by his sin, becomes also alienated from nature. Instead of being a steward under his Creator, he exploits nature and directs it to his own ends.

As a result, nature fails to cooperate with man, and the harmony of the garden is transformed into the chaos of the wilderness. Divinely enjoined to multiply and people the earth and to subdue it, man has carried out both injunctions without concern for the divine purpose. The result is a population burst and, at the same time, a mishandling of the earth's natural resources. Any true balance between man and nature is rapidly being destroyed.

In the fourth place, the Incarnation and Resurrection promise the redemption of nature as well as man, and the ultimate consummation has a cosmic dimension which we only too often ignore. Be it noted, however, that the redemption of man is primary. The new humanity is the center of the new creation, for the creation exists in part to provide the setting for man's fellowship with God, the new covenant. Let us remember also that we dare not presumptuously regard nature as solely created for man. It may well play a part in the divine purpose in its own right. The creation-tradition of the wise men, a layman's approach, occasionally indicates this and celebrates God's pleasure in the whole created order.

In the fifth place, since the redemption is already being wrought out within the historical scene, the renewal of man's relationship to nature is one dimension of the Church's redemptive mission. The salvation of the individual, with eyes mainly upon a transcendent and heavenly order, ignores the fact that the setting of this universe is straining forward expectantly for the final unveiling of the sons of God. But as already stated, the Christ makes such sonship available to historical man. Hence, it must be accompanied by the preparation of man's natural habitat for that final unveiling.

TWO

The Scientific Background of the Environmental Issue

THE BIBLICAL VIEW OF NATURE outlined in the preceding chapter is paralleled by the findings of the contemporary biological sciences. The fact that the ecological problem has become a central one for the years ahead is a direct result of intensive investigation in the past decades of the influence of environmental factors upon living organisms.

No one can approach the theological dimension of our environmental dilemma without an adequate understanding of what science is saying. It is not our purpose to go into technical discussions or to cite the arrays of scientific data which are available. Rather we shall emphasize the main insights which have guided and are central in contemporary ecology. In doing so, we must take account of such matters where they have peculiar significance for our theological interpretation and for ethical considerations. This involves some discussion of the understanding of the evolutionary process, as well as a consideration of the contemporary ecological situation. Before we begin a more detailed discussion we need to remember that the adjective "environmental" covers two significant dimensions.

34

All living things live in interdependence both with a physico-chemical context and with other living organisms. These will have to be considered in turn and so also will the whole issue of the reproduction of organisms within the matrix which nature provides. Finally we must look at the peculiar problems which are posed for such a general life setting by the human economy.

EVOLUTIONARY MODELS AND ENVIRONMENT

The developmental emergence of the species by an evolutionary process has become commonplace in scientific thought. So often, however, we forget that the models by which we have sought to understand the available data and to elucidate the mechanism behind the development have had a varied history. We have moved from the Lamarckian to the Darwinian model, and from the latter to the Neo-Darwinian, while a Neo-Lamarckian model occasionally makes itself felt in the wings of the scientific stage. That the Neo-Darwinian model is scientific orthodoxy by no means indicates that it satisfactorily explains all the data which nature provides. At the moment it seems the most viable, the more so when environmental factors are given more serious consideration than the laboratory setting of so many leading advocates has made possible. It is true to say that the natural historian or field naturalist needs also to be listened to when evolutionary issues are under consideration as well as the laboratory and experimental material which appropriately preoccupies the geneticists. This is increasingly being realized. As Marston Bates comments: "Students of evolution, certainly, are always preoccupied with the nature of the environment, with its changes, and with environmental adaptations. Yet they do tend to devote a great deal more attention to mechanisms within the organism, to the whole complex study that has come to be called 'genetics,' than they do to external, ecological considerations."[1]

The basic types of scientific model are both concerned with the interaction of the organism and its environment. Toynbee has suggested that human history moves forward on the basis of "challenge and response," and this phrase would appear to apply also to evolutionary change. The models are distinguished, however, by the roles played by the two partners in the developmental process. The

Lamarckian model sees the changes in the environment evoking
adaptive changes in the organism which are handed on to its descendants. Its emphasis on the inheritance of acquired characteristics has never been satisfactorily verified, although Neo-Lamarck-
ians are still to be found and, at one stage, this model was given
political authenticity by the Soviet government. Generally speaking,
it may be said to have been discredited scientifically, and this theory
of ectogenesis may be left on one side, yet there is still a lurking
fear of the "Lamarckist" in the scientific mind. Marston Bates has
gone so far as to suggest that this is a reason, generally an uncon-
scious one, why many geneticists have tended to cling to the laboratory and the investigation of what goes on in the organism, rather
than to pay more attention "to external, ecological considerations."[2]

This brings us to the Darwinian model. As first postulated by
Darwin himself, this model was inspired by Malthus' study of human populations. Its emphasis falls primarily upon the organism,
which is supposed to show at all times an array of small "chance"
variations. Normally such variations are of no value in helping the
organism to adapt itself to its environment. When, however, changes
occur in that environment, some variations may aid the organism
possessing them to adapt itself to its new context. In that case, nature tends to select the organisms possessing variations with such
survival value and to perpetuate their existence by the process of
heredity. Thus the two key phrases are "natural selection" and
"survival value." The emphasis on "chance" in Darwin's original
statement has often been misconstrued. He himself contended that
the word simply implied that he was not aware of the mechanism
by which such organismic variations appeared.

Since his time, we have learned much more about the mechanisms
of heredity. We know that the inherited characteristics of any organism are carried in its living cells by paired sets of chromosomes,
each consisting of complex molecular structures with constituent
genes. The last few years have seen us discovering the patterns of
these structures and identifying them as varying forms of the de-
oxyribonucleic acid molecule (DNA) with its double helix pattern.
We know a great deal about the coding of such bearers of heredity,
the way which, like miniature IBMs, they release appropriate mes-

sengers or enzymes to initiate in the growing organism the development of characteristic aspects which identify it with its forebears. The pioneer work of such investigators as Spencer Jennings and T. H. Morgan fifty years ago on chromosomes and their constituent genes launched biological science on a stream of genetical investigations which have issued today in the work of men like Dobzhansky, Darlington, Waddington, and Wilson. The last named was responsible for the solving of the structural mystery of the DNA molecule.

This concern with genetics and the inner working of the organism has unveiled one important factor in the evolutionary process. We know now that Darwin's small variations were wrongly identified by him and were mere superficial changes. The real factor in developmental change must be sought in mutations within the genetic molecules. Such random mutations in the seed cells give rise to offspring which manifest characteristics at variance with those of the parents. If they give their possessor greater survival value, they are preserved by a process of natural selection, and the changed characteristics are perpetuated in their descendants by heredity. As a succession of such small mutations takes place in the process of the generations, there emerges a new species quite distinct from that from which, generations earlier, it had issued by reproduction. Thus new species are the cumulative result of small mutations operated upon by natural selection. The environmental influences and changes are those which make such selection possible.

The tendency of geneticists has been to place the emphasis upon genetic mutations within the organism rather than upon the environmental factors. Increasingly, however, the significance of the latter and of natural selection has been reemphasized. Mutations are random and unpredictable. We know that they are caused when the genetic structures are subject to chemicals or high energy radiation. They are happening all the time in organisms in their natural surroundings, but their infrequent occurrence makes it difficult to understand the role they play unless we recognize the importance of population genetics. R. A. Fisher[3] and Th. Dobzhansky[4] have discussed statistically what happens in a population of similar organisms to an organism that possesses an adaptive advantage over its neighbors, however slight that advantage may be. They have shown that such an advantage profoundly affects the spread of this favorable genetic material throughout the population. Thus when account is taken of populations, we have a basis for the effect of advantageous mutations, however infrequently they may occur. Their selective advantage leads to their incorporation in the gene-complex of the whole, and it removes the necessity of a high mutation rate, an issue which beset Darwin's own approach.

The mechanism of cumulative micromutations under the operation of natural selection does not provide all the answers. It is difficult to understand how natural selection could be operative in the case of small mutations that cumulatively might make possible the emergence of the eye from an initial organism with only a light sensitive spot. The small mutations that the emergence of such a complicated structure would involve would seem to have little or no adaptive advantage on their own and in isolation from the other mutations necessary to produce the complex organ. Here the work of Fisher might well provide the answer. But it is significant that a Neo-Darwinian like Dobzhansky[5] now speaks of "quantum mutations," a phrase also used by G. G. Simpson.[6] The former refers, for example, to the necessary concomitance of a series of mutations which must have occurred together for man to emerge in the creative process—the upright stance, tools, the constant sexual receptivity of females, change in food habits, relaxation of male aggressiveness. He suggests that such changes occurred together with natural reinforcement and that the transition is novel in the sense that a completely new evolutionary pattern emerges.[7] He says that such "quantum mutations" are unlikely to involve changes of one trait at a time. The whole genotype or gene-structure and the whole external form or phenotype "are reconstructed to reach a new adaptive balance."[8] Such quantum mutations might therefore point to discontinuities in the process. The differences between the generations would increase so rapidly that they would be perceived as differences of kind.[9] However, the changes of gene structure would still be fundamental, while the environment would play a significant selective role. Like changes occurring on less favorable occasions would presumably not have been adaptive and would not have persisted.[10]

Other biologists would accept the micromutations/natural selection model within species but would see some other forces at work in the intraspecies movement. Dalcq speaks of ontomutations; von Bertalanffy uses the idea of orthogenesis; Goldschmidt refers to "systematic mutations" and the emergence of happy monsters; and so on.[11] Marston Bates significantly accepts the slow accumulation of small differences, microevolution, yet adds ". . . I still will suggest that the mutations, the variations, that lead to striking new directions in evolution, to the development of new orders, classes and phyla, may sometimes be of a different sort from the commonly observed minute variations."[12] Evidently there is no general agreement, although the scientific consensus favors the Neo-Darwinian model. What is important for us is the role played by the environment. Dobzhansky agrees that "evolution is, in part, ectogenesis; it is brought about by causes outside the organism, or, more precisely, through interactions between the organism and its environment. . . . The environment determines the changes which occur not directly but only by way of natural selection, a process first clearly expounded by Darwin."[13]

There are weak spots in the idea of natural selection itself. If we apply this model too literally and assume as valid what we see in adaptation at the human level, we find ourselves in difficulty. Mimicry in nature, such as an insect being structured with wings to look like a leaf, can be explained as camouflage, a mutation which is selected because of its protective significance. But when we realize that preying insects, predators, may be sensitive to ranges of light not available to the human eye, the visible resemblance is often shattered. Marston Bates cites the work of W. L. McAtee which demonstrated that insects supposed to have coloration which protected them were found in the stomachs of the predatory birds in the same proportion to their abundance as species of insects that were not so protected.[14] Actually many species survive quite successfully without a protective camouflage. This and other issues make it clear that natural selection must not be pressed too far. It is, at best, a useful analogue or model which helps us to understand something of the process.

Again, our Victorian forebears were often repelled at the thought of natural selection because it savored to them of "Nature, red in tooth and claw/With ravine" (to use Tennyson's phrase). In this they were encouraged by T. H. Huxley's understanding of Darwinism. But nature forms a cooperative system, as we shall note shortly, and there is much more cooperation in nature than internecine strife. This is especially evidenced in the work of field naturalists who study life in its natural habitat rather than in the artificial abstraction of a laboratory setting. The fact that the natural selection model applies to populations and not to individuals in isolation is a reminder that survival must be understood in terms of the group. There is no merciless struggle for life within a species. Rather, in the struggle for survival, there seems to be an attempt to avoid competition so far as possible. Nature is a harmonious system in which there is a mutual dependence and cooperation of living things.

Kropotkin,[15] exiled to Siberia in the days of Russian tsardom, accumulated much evidence to support this. He concluded that living organisms constitute a cooperative society in which the best is achieved for all in a given environment. L. Richmond Wheeler confirmed such a viewpoint by his field studies in Malaya. He sums up his conclusions as follows: "What has happened is that all living organisms, like a vast cooperative society which includes many smaller ones, have succeeded in adapting themselves, unconsciously of course in most cases but semi-consciously in some animals, to abundant and victorious life in all sorts of habitats according to the fitness of the local environment. Where this allows much life, there it is, in numerous individuals and species, astoundingly cooperative in space and time; where external conditions are less favorable, there again is the apparently maximum amount of life possible, at least in plants, on stony waste, in sun-scorched desert, in ocean depth of tremendous pressures, even on snow."[16]

All this suggests that the emphasis on chance and randomness should not lead to the rejection of an overall directiveness in the process.[17] The very balance and cooperativeness of the natural process indicates the presence of more than the chance turning of a roulette wheel. The suggestion that the major movements in the process may involve larger mutations, whether these be envisaged within the Neo-Darwinian model as with Dobzhansky's "quantum mutations" or by some as yet undiscovered mechanism as with Dalcq and others, would indicate again some teleological movement. Macroevolution suggests a long-time orderly progress, and some coordination of mutations, some mutual reinforcement, would appear to be a necessity. Polanyi, himself a capable scientist, suggests that consideration of long range evolutionary progress such as the development of the human consciousness requires more than random mutations with adaptive and reproductive advantages. The consecutive steps in such a movement would need a special type of adaptive advantage, one which contributed "to a continuous ascending evolutionary achievement." Hence, he sees a persistent creative trend under the operation of an orderly transforming principle.[18] Dobzhansky likewise, although not opposed like Polanyi to the accepted biological approach, can describe the adaptive responses of the organism in macroevolution as creative. The changes at this level of change are unpredictable and irreversible. They constitute "a creative response of living matter to environmental opportunity."[19] He ties up such creativity with the process itself, seeing the origination of novelties but also the risk of failure or nonfulfillment. However we look at the process, teleological interpretation keeps lifting its head, whether we look for large scale "miracles" or a large number of small wonders that mutually reinforce one another.[20] Somehow the evolving organism and its environment are built together into a cooperative and creative whole.

This brings us at once to the ecological issue. The part played by the environment in the long history of the creative development of living things is naturally continued in the present moment of human history when the species have become relatively stabilized.

ECOLOGICAL PATTERNS—THE CHEMICAL LIFE CYCLES

Over a half century ago, Professor Lawrence J. Henderson of Harvard University published an epoch-making book entitled *The Fitness of the Environment*. In it he examined the chemical factors in the environment and in living things, especially carbon dioxide and water, together with the significance of carbon. He concluded, after exhaustive analysis, that "the elements carbon, hydrogen, and oxygen are uniquely and most highly fitted to be the stuff of which life is formed and of the environment in which it exists."[21] He added that "no other environment consisting of primary constituents made up of the known elements, or lacking water and carbonic acid, could possess a like number of fit characteristics or such highly fit characteristics, or in any manner such great fitness to promote complexity, durability, and active metabolism in the organic mechanism which we call life."[22] Such numerous coincidences cannot be attributed to mere chance. They indicated, for Henderson, the presence of law. The way in which cosmic evolution works step by step with biological evolution suggests that the two streams of evolution are in some sense one, and that what appear to be contingent happenings really constitute a single orderly development "resembling those which in human action we recognize as purposeful."[23] This indication of teleological dimension in the physical process reinforces the suggestion already made that there is a like dimension in the mutations and the transformation of the species. At this point, however, we want to stress the emphasis on the fitness of the chemical constituents of our earthly environment and their function in the support of life.

Immediately we are brought face to face with the most fundamental factors in the ecological issue—the chemical life cycles. Ultimately there are only two sources of energy available for the origination and maintenance of life on our planet—solar energy and radioactivity. The latter, as we have seen, plays a part in the genetic mutations, but it is the energy of the sun, arriving on earth as radiation, which is the basic energy source for all life. One immediate way in which the sun affects us is in the temperature of our planet. Terrestrial life can exist only in a narrow belt of temperature from a few degrees above freezing to a maximum of $45°C$, and the optimum of life's efficiency is somewhere in the middle of this range. Here the geographical factor and the seasonal fluctuations of temperature come into play, while the constitution of the earth's atmosphere also plays an important part. Animals and plants alike release carbon dioxide into the atmosphere, and with the advent of man and modern technology, the amount of this gas is increased considerably. The human population-burst and the industrial waste tend to augment the percentage of carbon dioxide, while the accompanying destruction of plant life, which withdraws it from the atmosphere, tends to reduce the rate of withdrawal. In consequence, there can be a real danger that the changed construction of our atmosphere will form a stronger heat insulator and raise the temperature of our planet. Without technological man, however, nature, left to its own devices, has hitherto balanced itself.

Along with the heat factor, we also must count the light factor, without which life would be impossible. The whole range of solar radiation comes under this description—infrared to ultraviolet. The distribution and adaptation of organisms is in part determined by the seasonal fluctuations of daylight, and here again the geographical factor comes into play. Seasonal changes and geographical locations, with their accompanying variations of available light and of temperature, thus play a significant role in the existence and persistence of life in all its many forms. Any severe tampering with the constitution of our atmosphere would have serious repercussions.

A third aspect of our planetary environment at the physical level is the plentiful supply of water. The geological record shows that life began in the water. The oldest fossils that we possess are those of marine organisms. Significantly, all organisms appear to carry the mark of the seas in which life came to birth. They are primarily water, while the proportion of inorganic salts present in living matter or protoplasm approaches closely to that of their presence in sea water. Furthermore, all organisms, and not merely the aquatic ones, require water for life to continue. Land organisms depend so much upon it that important aspects of their physiology and behavior are concerned with the obtaining, retention, and economic use of water.

Not only is water a necessary constituent in the internal growth and structure of organisms, but its abundance or scarcity determines the type of organism in any geographical locale. It passes through the cycle of evaporation from the oceans, the formation of clouds, and precipitation in the form of rain or snow. Such precipitation depends upon the currents in the air, mountain ranges, and the like. Ultimately it finds its way back to the ocean either by streams and rivers or by seeping through the earth to the underground water table. Its scarcity or its abundance has a great effect upon the type of organism in any locality. Desert animals include creatures like lizards which never require water in a liquid state and camels which can exist for a considerable time without water. But most animals require a great deal of water. This is particularly true of those which perspire, for example, the horse. The presence of moisture in the air, humidity, provides yet another ecological factor.

If this supply of water is polluted by alien substances which destroy or reduce its dissolved oxygen content or which are poisonous to some or all living things, the consequence is disaster. Neither man nor his organic environment can exist without water.

This brings us to the primary chemical substances and their cycles in relation to living things. At the outset we need to remind ourselves that the basic groups of organisms in the life process are constituted by the flora. It is the existence of flora that has made possible the vast system of fauna in all its wide variety. All animals with a few exceptions ultimately depend upon the plants for their food. The basic elements in life are carbon, hydrogen, oxygen, and nitrogen. Added to these in fairly considerable quantity are chlorine, sulphur, phosphorous, sodium, potassium, silicon, calcium, iron, and magnesium. In all this, water is an important fact. All organisms get their necessary oxygen either from the atmosphere directly or from its solution in water. Again, all the other elements necessary for life, with the exception of carbon, are obtained by plants from the presence of salts in the soil or salts in solution in water. Furthermore, the hydrogen in water becomes a necessary constituent of the complex organic molecules which are central in the processes of living things.

The complex organic molecules are built around the chemical properties of carbon, and all the carbon in the organisms of this planet is derived from carbon dioxide. It is here that the plant life is so basic for the whole life process, for it is the focal point of the carbon cycle. Every living thing lives on the substance of other living things with the exception of the plants. The latter, whether leafy green plants on land or the smaller green plants in the plankton of water, are the primary sources of all food, and they depend entirely upon solar energy.

By their possession of chlorophyll, such plants are able to store solar energy and utilize it in combining their intake of water with carbon dioxide drawn from the atmosphere. This process is known as photosynthesis. In this way the carbon in the carbon dioxide is manufactured into sugars, fats, carbohydrates, and proteins which are constituents of the protoplasm of the plant. These plant-carbohydrates and plant-proteins provide the basic foods for the whole animal order, and so carbon becomes a constituent element of the animal body. The energy necessary for living is made available in the latter by a process of slow burning or oxidation, known as metabolism. In it the carbohydrates are oxidized and carbon dioxide is released into the air once more. Furthermore the decay of those plants which are not eaten, together with the dissolution of dead animal bodies, also discharges carbon dioxide into the atmosphere, while the combustion of organic matter adds additional amounts of the gas. Thus the carbon dioxide taken in by the plants is replenished as the cycle of nature follows its path. Let man, by technological processes and by destruction of plant life and forests, upset this natural balance and disaster may follow.

In the process of utilizing the solar energy and of manufacturing the complex organic molecules, the plants give off oxygen to the air. The water provides sufficient oxygen for the process of photosynthesis so that the carbon is taken from the carbon dioxide and the oxygen content of the latter is released. This oxygen is returned to the air around the green parts of the plant. It then becomes available for the slow burning or oxidation process of metabolism in all organisms. Even the plants require this in the night when photosynthesis cannot function and when they obtain energy by oxidizing their carbohydrates. The organisms take in the oxygen from their surroundings and release carbon dioxide in its place. Once more we have a cycle which nature keeps in balance. Oxygen is drawn in from the surroundings by the respiration of organisms to facilitate oxidation and returned by the plants in the process of photosynthesis. Once again nature maintains a balanced cycle.

The other chemical cycle is that of nitrogen. The free nitrogen in the atmosphere cannot be utilized directly like carbon dioxide and oxygen. It has to be converted into nitrites and nitrates so that the plants may use it for the manufacture of their proteins. This conversion is effected by bacteria which fix the nitrogen in chemical compounds in the soil and which are found around the roots of leguminous plants, like clover. Lightning also enables the combination of atmospheric nitrogen with oxygen and thus the formation of nitrates.

Nitrates are formed in the soil and made available to the plants by their solution in soil water. From the plants the nitrogen passes in the food process into animal bodies. The decay of plants, the excretion of animals, and the dissolution of dead animal bodies restores the nitrogen to the soil, where bacteria again get to work forming nitrates and releasing free nitrogen into the atmosphere.

We note that basic to the support of life are the plants and bacteria, for the prime agents in breaking up the organic matter of dead animal bodies and decaying plants as well as excretions are microbes set to pursue specific chemical functions. As we have just seen, bacteria are the significant factors in the nitrogen cycle. If they are in some way eradicated from the soil or reduced in quantity, the basic materials that make life possible could not be manufactured by the plants and passed on as food to the animal order.

We might seem to have suggested that the balance in these cycles is perfectly maintained by nature. This is, however, only relatively true. Particularly in the case of nitrogen, nature is continually in difficulty. There is a persistent leakage of nitrogen from salts in the soil into a gaseous form in the air. When insufficient oxygen is available, the bacteria that normally function in the formation of nitrates reverse their role, abstracting the oxygen from the nitrates and freeing the nitrogen into the atmosphere. Here the nitrogen is inert and unavailable for the support of life unless it makes contact with nitrogen-fixing bacteria which are closely associated with the leguminous plants. These alone can restore the balance and keep sufficient nitrogen in the soil available for the support of life. Peat, lignite, coal, and oil deposits are also reminders of the way nature puts blocks in the chemical cycles. These substances have put carbon out of circulation and kept it locked up in unavailable form for millions of years. Today modern technology is using them and restoring carbon to the atmosphere, but now it is the over-abundance of carbon dioxide that may threaten the natural processes.

These complicated climatic conditions and chemical cycles function in ultimate relation to the whole living environment, plants and animals. This structure of life must now be studied in more detail.

THE BIOLOGICAL ENVIRONMENT AND THE ECOLOGICAL PYRAMID

Ecologists have developed a special vocabulary in their approach to nature. Living organisms in any area form a closely inter-connected whole in which many species are involved, both animals and plants. Such communal groupings are known as biotic communities. The individual species involved in such groupings are styled populations. Each kind of organism has further its own particular locale. This is known as its habitat. Such a habitat will be both physical and organic. Organisms live in specific types of physical environment, such as soil or water, but they also may be closely associated with other living things in the life process. Furthermore, each species serves a peculiar function within the communal structure, and this is described as its niche.

Every biotic community consists of a hierarchy of populations. There are green plants as food producers, plant-eating animals or herbivores which live on the plants, possibly carnivorous animals which live on the flesh of other animals, and the bacteria which hasten the decay of dead plants and animal bodies and break down their contents into available forms. Each organismic population fills its niche in the community and fulfills its role or function. It is an interesting thing to trace the food chains of such a community, beginning with the plants, moving on to the animals which feed on the vegetation, and so to those animals which prey upon such herbivores, the predators.

We often speak of the ecological pyramid which does represent in diagrammatic form what we have been discussing. At the base we have a mass of plant life, consisting of many different populations, some of them in active competition, but all providing food for the next stage of the hierarchy. Some of these populations will be dominant, such as oaks in an oak forest or grass in a field. Others will be less abundant, but will manage to fulfill their role (or fill their niche) within the margin of opportunity left to them by the dominant species. The dominant species will be the ones which can get the biggest share of the solar energy available in the habitat of the community. This results in their being the tallest vegetation. The other plant populations live under the shadow of the dominant ones and make do with the solar energy that can reach them.

The next level of the pyramid consists of large numbers of herbivores, from insects like earth worms and grasshoppers to creatures like rabbits, sheep, and deer; the variety of populations varying according to the habitat. Here, too, each fills its niche, some being more dominant than others. The predators and carnivores live upon the herbivores which provide their food. They form the third level of the pyramid structure and include insects like spiders, dragonflies, and ladybirds; birds like swallows, hawks, and eagles; animals like lions, tigers, and wolves. Again, each population will fill its niche and perform a significant role within the whole. Also one or a few of the populations will be dominant. Thus a biotic community may be capped with a population of creatures powerful enough not to be preyed on in its turn—lions, for example. We have to add to these groups the presence of scavengers like earthworms, vultures, and jackals. These work around the fringe of the biotic community disposing of its refuse in decaying plants and dead animal remains.

It is easy to see such a community as filled with intense competition, gory with the struggle for survival. Marston Bates, however, disputes this view first held by T. H. Huxley. He contends that the biotic community "is a functioning unit, and the various component populations serve to build up the unit as a whole."[24] Whereas many emphasize the presence of predators and parasites, Bates would argue that intracommunal relationships have a cooperative aspect even here. The cat preys upon the mouse, but the mouse proliferates much more abundantly so that the predatory activity of the cat provides population control and balance. Without such control, the density of the mouse population would militate against its best interests. In addition, the cats benefit by food supply.[25]

Again, Bates draws attention to the mutual dependence of plants and animals. The plants provide the animals with food, but themselves benefit because the animals are able to move and thus disperse and fertilize the plants. Insect pollination affords one example. The random mechanism of wind distribution is not sufficient to explain the development of a complex plant community, whereas the mobility of insects probably accounts for much of this.[26] Under such terms as symbiosis, mutualism, and commensalism, biologists have discussed in great depth the relationships of living things from the level of mutual dependence to the level of unilateral dependence. Thus the sea anemone which attaches itself to the shell of the hermit crab provides the crab with camouflage and at the same time gets free transport to areas where the food supply is abundant. Such mutualism is matched by a case of commensalism where the king crab carries a flatworm on its gills and appears to receive no benefit, whereas the flatworm feeds on particles of the crab's prey.

What is evident is that biotic communities are able to function as relatively self-sufficient wholes because of the interdependence and cooperation of the constituent populations. Thus a forest with its different populations of trees, its wide variety of bird populations, its insects, and so on, each group filling its particular niche, forms a functioning and fairly self-sufficient whole. Bates[27] points out that the communal life pattern associated with a pool in such a forest might be so tied in with the life of the forest itself that it could not be regarded apart from this larger environment. In that case, the biological groupings around the pool would have to be regarded as fulfilling a niche in the biotic community of the forest. In studying the life of the pool we must continually refer to the biological structures in the forest community.

Not all niches in biotic communities are filled. Indeed, such communities are usually in precarious balance. This depends essentially upon the way in which the role of reproduction of the constituent populations can be kept in proper proportion by environmental resistance. Thus, elephants have a slow rate of reproduction, although by size, habits, protective tusks, mammalian physiology, and so on, they are impervious to foes that might otherwise keep them from overbreeding. Other populations are kept from overabundant proliferation by the presence of sufficient predators. Climatic changes can, however, change the structures of relationship and destroy the

balance. Above all, human intervention, undertaken without sufficient understanding, can be disastrous. One outstanding example
was the introduction of the sparrow into the United States from
England. In England, it had sufficient natural predators to keep
overreproduction in check and was useful in dealing with insect pests.
In America, its introduction was on the basis of its latter role—keeping down the insect pests which were destroying Boston's shade trees.
But, in this country, it was free of its natural enemies, and it has now
so proliferated that it has become a pest itself, feeding on grain crops,
preying on the other insect-eating birds. We shall look at the DDT
problem shortly. Elliott comments: "We can tamper with the environment only in small areas for specific purposes; any large-scale
operation must be carried out with utmost caution so that the balanced plan of the community of animals is not disturbed."[28]

SUMMING UP

In no scientific description do we expect to meet the idea of God
or the concept of purposive direction. Science is not concerned with
what is transcendent, and it concentrates on efficient causes. Its
emphasis is on what is sensibly observable, and its basic categories
are tied to models which do not have an immediate teleological
reference. It needs to be noted, however, that teleological categories
do continually lift their heads in the biological sciences despite re-
ductionist efforts to make the study of life simply a study of physics
and chemistry. There is an increasing group of scientists who advo-
cate that biology should build up its own basic categories and that
here teleology cannot be ignored.

We have sought to show that the process of evolution indicates,
even at the scientific level, some degree of creative directiveness.
Furthermore, this directiveness arises out of a close interrelationship
between the organism and its environment in which cooperation as
well as competition is present. A careful study of the ecological data
supports the view that there is a sustained balance in nature in which
organisms live in close relationship to one another and to their
physical environment. While it is true that such a balance is often
precarious and that biological niches or roles are by no means wholly
filled in any biotic community, there is much evidence to support the

idea which the Hebrews, lacking our scientific knowledge, sought to express in their covenant idea. They did, of course, introduce the religious motif, and this the scientist qua scientist cannot do. Yet science on its own, and apart from religious coloring, does reveal a cooperative balance. Even the competitive aspect, manifest in the various food chains of a biotic community, should not make us close our eyes to the fact that the life process is built into a series of ordered and cooperative wholes. That man has upset such balance in a way that subhuman predators, however dominant, never do, is a matter to which we must now turn our attention.

THREE

Man—the Predator

WITH THE EMERGENCE OF MAN, this world-process became conscious of itself. What Dobzhansky has called a "quantum mutation" and Dalcq, an "ontomutation," took place, and there came a being who was characterized by self-awareness. It is true that behavioristic psychologists tend to ignore such a description and follow their reductive techniques in describing consciousness and self-consciousness. But responsible scientists, and biologists in particular, are increasingly emphasizing the uniqueness and real distinctiveness of this emergent quality: A dog knows but it does not know that it knows. When man emerges within the process, we find a being who is aware of his processes of reflection and shows the marks of self-transcendence.

Man is able to turn himself into an object and to become aware of his own "I-ness." Dobzhansky points out that Rensch finds the rudiments of this in the animal order but "affirms emphatically that a fully developed self-awareness is diagnostic of humanity."[1] He notes that the words "self-awareness" and "self-objectification" are now becoming legitimized, and cites current psychological and sociological opinion. Human social existence acquires meaning for the individual through self-awareness. Especially this is evident at the level of the moral order and in man's unique capacity for reflective thought, his ability to recognize universal meanings and values and to appropriate them for himself. Hellowell states that "an organized social life in man, since it transcends purely biological and geographical determinants, cannot function apart from communally recognized meanings and values, or apart from the psychological structuralization of individuals who make these their own."[2]

W. H. Thorpe reminds us that man is distinctively separated from the animal order by his capacity to appraise absolute values. He finds the roots of many of the mental characteristics of human behavior at the animal level, including altruism, cooperativeness, and language. But in every case he finds a dividing line when such potential capacities are harnessed to the conscious pursuit of absolute values. He comments, early in his argument, that "this is something which far transcends anything we have reason to believe exists in the animals. Here there seems to be a dividing line indeed."[3] Man seeks for the truth, pursues the beautiful, and strives to attain the good. In the creative evolutionary process this capacity for absolute values has come with that emergence of self-transcendence which characterizes man as personal being. In the light of these, reflective thought, creative artistry, and moral behavior became possible. They lift man above the process, enable him to transcend it. Indeed they are the marks of his freedom. Yet tragically that freedom also makes it possible for him to deny his absolute values, choose lesser and often evil ends, and mishandle the very process of nature from which he has emerged.

SCIENTIFIC AND MORAL VALUES

When man first emerged, he found himself surrounded by mystery and often battling with his environment. Certain characteristic forms of behavior began to manifest themselves, forms that we should describe as human—the religious response, the response associated with primitive magic, and the moral response. Judging by the drawings of early cave man and the early accompaniments of religious practice, there was also an artistic response. In the religious response we have the vague awareness of a mysterious and transcendent presence which must in some way be propitiated so that its assistance and power might offer to man some measure of security. It is not our business to argue whether primitive monotheism may be postulated as initially present or whether the idea of mana prevailed. What is probably true is that there was a primitive sense of the holy, in Otto's sense of a mystery which strangely allured and yet evoked creaturely fear, a mystery to be placated by sacrifice and prayer. With this came the moral response. Again, how far the moral was associated with the religious response may well be a matter of debate. What is clear is that moral tabus were early formulated, guiding man's human relationships and his treatment of nature. Yet again, we have the response of magic, the attempt to compel nature to cooperate by spells and runes in contrast with the persuasive and appeasing approach of religion. Here, too, it would seem that primitive man did not differentiate between religion and magic, but that both modes of behavior were closely intertwined. Already man was showing his capacity for absolute values which he regarded as binding on himself and his society. All his responses to reality were specially concerned with his communal life and his natural environment. The changing seasons; the supply of food; the mysteries of rain and sunshine, of darkness and light, of storm and calm; the mysteries of birth and death; the mysteries of sex—man, striving to be man and not to lose himself in the nature from which he had emerged, had to deal with all of these and many more.

As civilization developed, magic gave way to more rational ways of understanding and controlling the environment and of dealing with natural phenomena. Modern science has grown out of this more rational response and thus is the replacement of magic. Religion passed through the stage of mythmaking to develop a rationale along the lines of reflective thought, while still retaining its use of myth and symbols. Philosophical thought developed its own more abstract and rational approach to ultimate reality. Morality, at first closely bound up with religion, also moved into an autonomous status, although religion still retained its ethical dimension. Man the amphibian, immersed in nature and yet transcending it, increasingly sought to control his environment and direct it to his own purposes. But he was also becoming increasingly aware of absolute claims and universal obligations which overrode the urge for self-preservation that was part of his animal heritage. The animal appetites are concerned with private satisfaction, but with man there emerges the wide sense of universal obligation. Man's pursuit of truth is undertaken under the pressure to attain a rational understanding of reality at whatever cost. The claims of altruism and the concern for others, the moral obligations that overrode family, tribal, and even national loyalties, were increasingly recognized.

When man first emerged, he had a capacity to respond to claim and obligation. This was one aspect of the new quality of the personal and self-transcendent which characterized his being. But then absolute claims and obligations gathered content within the process of history. As man developed within the temporal movement, he became more aware of the content of moral claim and more sensitive to the obligation to seek for goodness and truth, which undergirded his morality and his scientific and philosophical pursuits. Above all, he moved to deeper understanding of the transcendent presence to which all religious experience points. For religion is the all-embracing response to the absolute, in which the totality of the person is involved. It, at its highest, requires the commitment of the whole man in his intellectual, moral, imaginative, and creative dimensions as well as at the level of feeling. Tillich can define religion as ultimate concern, that which grips a man in his totality because this concern transcends and yet embraces all the partial concerns which are present in human existence. It is concern that strikes at the roots of his creaturely and finite being, concern for that mystery which meets him in absolute demand and final succor, to use H. H. Farmer's description of the approach of God to man. Rudolf Otto sought the distinctive religious judgment in the appraisal of a numinous presence and mystery which struck fear and yet strangely allured, a *mysterium tremendum et fascinans*. In his analysis of religious experience, he sought to block out the rational and moral dimensions and arrive at a unique evaluation. Yet he had to restore those dimensions by a clumsy and sadly distorted Kantian mechanism. What H. D. Lewis and C. A. Campbell have suggested is much more apropos. Even fear and love or attraction are human feelings and become "felt analogies" when used to describe our experience of God. But they do not cover all of man's response to the divine—the "felt analogies" drawn from moral obligation and the passion for truth are also drawn to a focus in the transcendent presence.

All of human history testifies to the pressure for human excellence at all levels which activates human endeavor. Polanyi[4] has made the point that scientific discovery and indeed the pursuit of all truth require personal involvement. So-called objectivity is elusive, and we need to escape from the prison house of objectively demonstrable assertions, of positivistic preoccupation with objectivity. This is not a retreat into subjectivism, for Polanyi places great stress on what he calls the tacit dimension of knowing. He finds that basic to all knowledge is an often vague awareness of wholes which is prior to the consideration of the parts. Man is intuitively aware of some whole in reality and, on the basis of this tacit awareness, he moves out to discover some pattern among the particular aspects of reality which will fill in the awareness with comprehension. This primary awareness is focused upon the objectively given, and the investigation of the parts is thus seeking for a coherent pattern which will fill in the tacit knowing with explicit and articulate understanding. Polanyi holds that man always knows more than he can tell. In other words, our articulate knowledge is always expressed within an intuited framework which we cannot completely communicate. The pursuit of truth is the striving to weave the particulars of experience into a meaningful and coherent pattern.

Now this pursuit of truth means personal involvement. Imagination and intuitive hunches are brought into play in the search for a meaningful pattern to give comprehension to the tacit knowing. Aesthetic judgment also comes into play in science. Science is the result of a heuristic passion, a desire to discover truth and meaning. The scientist is, at his best, committed to a faith in the rationality of the universe. He is motivated by a heuristic passion in which he believes himself to be meeting eternal and universal obligations. "Science," Polanyi writes, "exists only to the extent to which there lives a passion for its beauty, a beauty believed to be universal and eternal."[5] He sees the matrix for such a pursuit of knowledge as provided by tacit assent, heuristic intellectual passion, cultural heritage, and a like-minded community. The emphasis on community means that the degree of objectivity attained is bound up with a community that shares a like heuristic passion. In all this, a faith principle is operative. The scientist is a committed man, and his basic beliefs are indubitable only in the sense that he believes them to be so.[6] There can be no claim of self-evidence. Polanyi defines his ultimate belief as "I believe that in spite of the hazards involved, I am called upon to search for the truth and state my findings."[7] Here is a declaration of absolute value.

Thus science partakes of the quality associated with religious response, moral obligation, and artistic vision. It has a quality of compulsion and obligation. It demands commitment to a goal that transcends personal ambition, private desires, and selfish ends. Its intellectual valuations are closely akin to moral judgments, and the heuristic passion of the scientist matches the thirst for righteousness that is basic in the moral sphere. Both alike find satisfaction in their capacity for enriching the world. The artist joins them at this point in his search for beauty and harmony. Overarching all, the religious man would see the claims of the deity in whom all absolute values cohere. All are men under claim.

This claim of religion was very evident in the medieval period when all culture was built around the Gothic cathedral with its spire pointing like a finger up to God. Men's pursuits of truth, artistic creativity, and moral concern were motivated by the faith that all such had their goal in God. From the Renaissance on, however, and still more radically in the period since the Enlightenment, the various pursuits have become autonomous and have drawn apart. It is significant that the early scientists—Galileo, Francis Bacon, René Descartes, Isaac Newton, Robert Boyle, John Ray, and many others—were men of deep religious conviction. They believed that in their scientific pursuit they were tracing the mind of the Creator. This meant that their discoveries were accompanied by genuine moral concern. We find Boyle refusing to publish the ingredients of some poisons; Sir Isaac Newton caustically condemning the announcement of a certain Oxford professor that his father had completed an invention for making artillery more destructive; Michael Faraday, when consulted by the British government as to the use of poison gas, declaring such to be inhuman and that he would have nothing to do with it. The heuristic passion for scientific truth marched hand in hand with moral obligation.

But since that day science has increasingly gone its own way and often been harnessed to materialistic and naturalistic world views. Morality also has detached itself from religious sanctions and moved into an autonomous development, associating itself likewise with naturalistic ideas. The moral absolute has been reduced to the utilitarian goals of Bentham and Mill or the evolutionary ideas of Herbert Spencer. Moral behavior has been accounted for in terms of social pressures or evolutionary survival mechanisms or Freud's superego as an imposed father image.

Often scientists have ventured into the moral field and advocated a naturalistic base for ethical conduct—T. H. Huxley, Julian Huxley, C. H. Waddington,[8] to name three. For Waddington, ethics is completely bound up with social need; it is an organ of society. He accounts for absolute values on social grounds by ascribing man's acceptance of authority to a natural process. Human society produces a sociogenetic system for transmitting and accepting information between the generations. As the solipsism of early babyhood breaks up, man is conditioned for an illusory belief in absolute and transcendent claim. We would not deny that society provides the realm in which absolute claim attains content, but the experience of unconditioned obligation cannot easily be reduced to a desire for more affection, stronger altruism, and more extensive sympathy. Julian Huxley implies that ethical issues can be solved by studying the course of evolution, but, as W. H. Thorpe points out,[9] he still can argue that morality guides men to "moral nobility of personality, a sense of oneness with something beyond and larger than ourselves, which is itself either moral or transcends and includes morality." Once absolute values are denied and relativity of values takes their place, it becomes increasingly difficult for scientific pursuits

to possess any authoritative voice in pointing to the social consequences of scientific discovery.

Man has all through history manifested the presence of a
demonic twist in his make-up, a tendency to reject absolute claim
and to turn his back on unconditional obligation. History is full
of man's self-interest and arrogance. Continually, final ends have
been replaced by the motivations of self-interest. Exploitation of
the environment and exploitation of his fellows have accompanied
man's historical existence. He has sought for lower and selfish
goals, replaced altruism and self-sacrifice by self-centeredness, sub-
stituted arrogance for humility, assumed the role of the exploiter
rather than the role of the servant. He has sought to be the center
of his world and to make his fellows and nature into means for his
own ends.

Of all misnomers, the ascription of *Homo sapiens* to man is one
of the greatest, for all through his history man has shown himself
far from wise in his treatment of his environment. It would appear
that historically the mishandling of the environment became a
more vital issue when man moved from the early stage of hunting
for wild animals and gathering wild plants to the pastoral and
agricultural stage of culture. In the early stage, man's average
intelligence was as high as now; he was developing his tools,
forming social structures, even practicing a rudimentary art. But
such men of the Stone Age lived close to their natural environment
and found in it their ecological niche. Man had become the chief
but also an adaptable predator. Even increasing ability in making
and inventing weapons still allowed him to remain within the
balance of nature. Then the pastoral and agricultural phase in
human history appeared. Somewhere in the seventh millenium B.C.,
man began to cultivate his own food—animal and plant. Agricultural methods and the raising of livestock transformed the face
of nature. Wild vegetation was replaced by cultivated food plants.
Browsing livestock began to graze in the tall grassy vegetation, and
wild game were driven from their fastness. A new biotic community began to appear, and the old eco-systems were pushed to the
uncivilized areas. The biological environment began to be re-
shaped by man, sometimes with a complete lack of wisdom. With

small human populations, man could move from an area where he had used up all the potential fertility of the soil or where he had stripped the vegetation by the raising of livestock, often leaving a desert behind him. Wisdom and intelligence could prevail. This, for example, is manifested in ancient laws that require that land be left fallow periodically. But such laws were often violated when human greed dominated a community. Professor G. L. Stebbins comments that "natural biotic communities all over the earth bear scars of wounds inflicted upon them by men for centuries or millennia, and these scars are continually becoming larger and uglier."[10]

Thus we do not face a new situation today but only one so aggravated that it has become critical. In a secular order, with religion largely bypassed and morality reduced to naturalistic levels, it is easier for modern man to evade the moral implications of his conduct, not only in his treatment of his fellows but also in his attitude toward his natural environment. The latter issue is the easier because morality has rarely said much about man's relation to nature and religion has often been preoccupied with the otherworldly.

So we face our present ecological crisis. Let it be said at once that there are many dedicated scientists whose heuristic passion in the pursuit of truth has not been marred by lesser goals and who have a genuine moral concern about the technological use to which their discoveries may be put. We have only to think of that large group of scientists who expressed their moral indignation at the use to which the discoveries of nuclear physics were being put in atomic warfare. In January 1958, a petition urging that the testing of nuclear bombs be stopped was signed by 9235 scientists, including leading American, British, and Russian scholars, and was presented to the United Nations. It included the words: "We have in common with our fellow-men a deep concern for the welfare of all human beings. As scientists we have knowledge of the dangers involved and therefore a special responsibility to make those dangers known."[11] The truth is that there are also many scientists who are not thus morally responsible or even scientifically responsible. Research can often be harnessed to lower ends than the absolute concern for the truth. Economic ends and industrial exploitation can mar the vision. Those who research in pesticides, cancer producing compounds, and the like have sometimes remained silent and not published results of their scientific investigation.

Yet the scientist is obligated to pursue the truth and make his discoveries known. We have no right to set limits upon the heuristic passion that should motivate scientific investigation nor to deny its absolute obligation to pursue the truth wherever it leads. Dr. Condon declared after the Second World War: "Whether scientific knowledge is used for good or evil purposes is a matter that is not part of science itself, but it is a matter of the deepest moral concern to scientists who are human beings having the same moral responsibilities and same responsibilities as citizens as have other people. Therefore, we cannot escape the necessity of giving thought and effort to the conditions under which science and scientists make their contribution to the world's progress."[12] How right he is! Man is more than a scientist and an inventive technologist. He is a morally responsible being. The torture of the modern scientist is that he is caught in a welter of claims which play upon us all. Many are relative—economic, class, racial, national. But others are absolute—moral duty, scientific obligation to the truth, the religious demands of divine love. It is just here that conscience should come into play. We have an obligation to publish scientific truth, whatever its possible applications. But we also have a moral obligation to point out the social consequences that may accrue.

Today the situation is being aggravated by the ecological issue, as if nuclear warfare were not a big enough issue on its own. What can the honestly committed scientist do? Many whose ethics are at best humanistic and more often naturalistic are showing genuine moral concern. We need to rediscover the realm of absolute values, though it may be wishful thinking for it to happen very much in our secular order. But advocates of the absolute, religious men and moralists, need to team up with humanists and naturalists in the recognition of a scientific obligation. Scientists are becoming increasingly aware of the way in which their scientific discoveries might be employed by and affect human society. They realize more than ever their involvement in social structures. In the McCarthy era, it was often claimed that "scientists should be on tap, but not on top." That false dictum can no longer be cited by responsible statesmen.

One thing is clear. The scientist must accept his role as teacher. His role is to teach humanity, not to govern. This is what Sir Thomas More described as the vocation of the single-minded man in 1516.[13] It still holds! The scientist cannot govern society, but he has a moral duty to teach society the implications and values involved in his discoveries. He has the responsibility to move beyond the heuristic pursuit of knowledge for its own sake and to indicate the moral and human consequences that may attend the use and misuse of his work. He can no longer remain neutral and have no concern for the technological developments attendant upon his findings.

There is a spirit of expediency present in government and industry which is absent from science. Science has always been grounded in a spirit of tolerance. Its Christian heritage cannot here be ignored, for it arose within the Christian tradition. It pursues its path with a sense of dignity, of devotion to the truth wherever it leads, of appreciation for human worth. Governments tend to be dominated by ideological concerns, to distort the truth for national purposes, to prostitute personal values to political and impersonal ends. Industry is harnessed to the urge for profits, the naked and unashamed pursuit of economic gain. This spirit often activates the whole personnel of an industrial concern, including its research scientists. Even the public is conditioned by the mass media to believe that the end of human existence is the accumulation of more and more things.

Science, with its empirical spirit, seeks humbly to measure its models against the brute reality of the given, of nature. The scientist must stand for such a spirit in a world where often the "powers that be" will want him "to be on tap, but not on top." The rules that apply to governments and the capitalistic enterprise seem to have little place for tolerance, the empirical attitude, the respect for nature, the service of the truth—all of which are central in the scientific approach to reality. Science has an ecumenical spirit which rises above economic rivalries and national barriers. At this point the scientist must make his contribution to the social and economic structures and the international fabric, the more so because government bureaucracies and industrial corporations will increasingly harness his discoveries to technological developments. Political and economic man tends increasingly to foul his own nest with little moral concern. Votes and profits count more than the future of humanity! Thus the scientist is required to do more than pursue natural truth. He has to take another value stance also, the moral. He must make his conscience evident in the common life. His approach and spirit are, at their best, more essentially humane and ecumenical than the machinery built by politics and economics, and he needs to make them felt. This is very evident, fortunately, in the increasing volume of scientific protest to our environment pollution. The pressures of the population burst and the ecological rape are bringing us to a crisis, where all men of good will need to cooperate.

The Environmental Problem

We must turn now from the relation of morality and science to the evident breakdown of any positive relation in our treatment of man's natural environment. The multifarious dimensions of this issue will be treated in the following analysis. Since the literature on this is voluminous, we will forgo much in the way of detail, but the footnotes will indicate sources which may be consulted. Our concern here is with the theological dimensions of the problem, and we propose therefore to indicate the main points at which the process of ecological rape is becoming focalized. It is here that Christian and non-Christian, religious man and secular man, humanist and naturalist, will have to learn cooperative action. Their motivation will be different, but they will agree in being concerned to redress the evils that we have wrought on that nature from which mankind has emerged. In the next two chapters we shall discuss what the theological attitude and Christian motivation should be. At this stage let us turn our attention to the indubitable facts that threaten man's future on this planet.

First of all, we begin at the inner structure of nature itself and look at the chemical cycle which is labeled the carbon cycle but which also involves the replenishment of oxygen in our atmosphere. Here several factors are at work. Sprawling urban growth has meant the destruction of vegetation and thus a reduction in the fundamental process of photosynthesis whereby carbon is abstracted from the air and oxygen returned to it. Industrial exploitation of forest timber, misuse of land which robs it of fertility, strip mining with its rape of the fertile soil have all added their quota to the reduction of our plant population. This means that more carbon dioxide remains in the atmosphere. To this we must add the tremendous increase in carbon dioxide due to industrial combustion and the burning of gasoline in internal combustion engines—automobiles, propeller and jet motivated airplanes, etc. In addition, the population burst means that more carbon dioxide is breathed into the atmosphere.

The other side also has to be noted. The oxygen content of the atmosphere is reduced as industrial combustion uses more, and the increase in the human population requires more oxygen for life itself. We have to remember that the free oxygen released in photosynthesis is used up again by the plant if we include its period of decomposition after death, so at this level there is no build-up of the free oxygen in the atmosphere. But industrial and private combustion is reducing that oxygen content and replacing it by carbon dioxide. This is the significant problem for the human race, for scientists fear its effect upon the world's climate. Carbon dioxide absorbs infrared rays but allows the energy-giving visible and ultraviolet rays from the sun to pass through. Now, if a large proportion of the gas is present in our atmosphere, it will not only shut out heat from the sun but also shut our earth-produced heat in. The consequences may produce floods as the earth's temperature rises and the polar icecaps melt, or a partial melting of the icecaps with attendant evaporation, snow storms and a new glacial age. Whichever is true, the scientists see dire results and especially condemn our use of fossil fuel in our burgeoning industrial complexes and transport systems.

Second, we have the water cycle. Here again there are many factors in the pollution of our water supply. The population burst has served to magnify the problem of the disposal of sewage, and much of that sewage has been dumped untreated into streams, rivers, and lakes. Again, the vast industrial enterprise of the modern world has meant the contamination of our natural water systems by all kinds of industrial waste. Yet again, our water supplies are being poisoned by insecticides which do not decompose quickly but retain their poisonous properties over a long span of time. Sprayed on the land, they find their way by rains, springs, and natural drainage into our streams and rivers and ultimately into the ocean. DDT is only *one* outstanding example, for persistent pesticides of other types still flow from the world's chemical companies even though DDT itself is increasingly banned.[14] Finally, especially in our oceans, we have the leakage of crude oil, fossil fuel, from wells sunk on the continental shelf, and the subsequent pollution of our sea water and our beaches.

What is all this doing? The Rienows have taken the situation in Afghanistan and applied it to that in America. They note that, in Afghanistan, "not only are the surface waters laden with diseases and plagues, but the lack of proper sewage disposal over the centuries has caused permeation by pollution of the sparse soils until the deep aquifer—that vast and mystical lake of fresh water underlying the earth's surface—has become universally contaminated."[15] They foresee a time when in America, too, the earth will have gone septic. ". . . to live in a country where the very soil in our garden and the ground water under our feet, put there over millions of years, are writhing with cholera, hepatitis, tuberculosis, typhus, dysentery, typhoid, diphtheria, polio, viruses, and hundreds of other plagues—where to drill a well in one's backyard is to challenge early death—must indeed be the ultimate horror. Mother Earth herself is then septic, sick unto death; decontamination is physically impossible."[16] Their gloomy prognostication is extreme, but there are more immediate consequences much closer home. Lake Erie[17] is in a more advanced stage of a doom that threatens the whole superb fresh water system of the Great Lakes. Industrial waste has been pumped into the lake for decades from the vast conglomeration of technological establishments on its shores. Senator Gaylord Nelson has described the lake as a chemical tank. Full of chlorides and other chemicals, its fish content dying rapidly and becoming inedible where it still survives, Lake Erie is in its death throes. It is being strangled for lack of oxygen. It is a terrible thing that the accumulating pollution in its waters is excluding the free oxygen that such waters hold in solution and upon which fish or other living things in the waters depend. No fish and no drinking water are possible in a chemical tank!

The same situation is exemplified in the Houston Ship Canal, another highly industrialized waterway, the bed of which is covered by oozy sludge, the accumulation of years of irresponsible dumping of industrial refuse. The canal is said to be the most polluted waterway in the world. Dissolved oxygen in the water and the associated sea life have disappeared and the "chemical tank" is spilling out into Galveston Bay, threatening one of the richest breeding grounds of the Gulf of Mexico. In particular, the rich oyster beds of Galveston Bay were threatened with mercury poisoning caused by waste from the manufacture of vinyl phonograph records, but were saved by timely research and also the warning of a Japanese tragedy. The latter took place at Minamata Bay, where deposited manufacturing waste was absorbed by the oysters and passed into the human beings around the bay. The oysters were able to absorb the mercury-bearing toxic effluent from industry and remain outwardly the same, but the humans who ate them went down with disastrous mercury poisoning.[18]

DDT is a persistent pesticide which does not rapidly decompose.[19] It is pouring into our oceans from our soil and decimating the fish life on our continental shelves. Off Pensacola, Florida, the use of this chemical to kill dogflies on the dried seaweed piled up on the beaches brought death to sea fish and sea birds alike for a two hundred mile stretch of coast.[20] Mosquito control programs have reduced the shrimp yield off parts of our coasts, and DDT in the ocean has almost brought about the extinction of sea birds like the Bermuda Petril by making their eggshells brittle.[21] Sea life is apparently much more susceptible to pesticides and less able to produce resistant mutations, but still predatory man continues on his irresponsible way.

Fresh water and sea water—all alike suffer. Indeed, many scientists declare that our oceans are dying. Paul Ehrlich[22] can write a scenario prophesying the end of the ocean by 1979 and stressing the way DDT slows down photosynthesis in marine plant life and will ultimately change destructively the whole eco-system. Marx[23] points to the occurrence of the red tides off the Florida Gulf Coast. These consist of members of the plankton family (labeled *Gymnodinium breve*) which produce a lethal effect on fish by the excretion of a nerve toxin. These tides have led to the extermination of millions of fish. Their cause has been traced to the effect on the normally life-giving plankton of fertilizers which are sent down into the ocean from Florida's soil by excessive rains. Nutrient chemicals like these fertilizers upset the balance and produce undue amounts of a member of the plankton which normally serves a positive role in this food chain. The toxic effect of the red tides has affected the oyster beds which accumulate the toxin. The oysters, when eaten, have dire effects on human beings. Similar red tides, composed of different kinds of plankton but equally toxic, are occurring off the California coast. The ocean is being poisoned!

As if all this is not enough, we have contamination of our sea water and beaches by oil gushing from leaks and by unsafeguarded oil wells sunk on our continental shelves. Here again the sea birds, as well as the beauty of nature itself, are the victims. Once more the ecological balance is upset.

Third, we turn to the nitrogen cycle. Here several problems arise. We have learned to use our fertile soil better, but we need to watch the soil mantle which has been spread around our earth across millions of years. With the development of civilization that top soil has been continually exploited. We need to leave it fallow for it to be renewed with nutrients, but food requirements of today's burgeoning population make it impossible to allow sufficient time to elapse for such renewal to take place. We are manufacturing artificial fertilizers, but to stave off famine, especially in the undeveloped countries, we need to produce above forty million tons a year. At the present time the world produces only about six million tons. Add to this the continual erosion of the valuable top soil by windstorms and by water, and the problem accumulates. Every year valuable soil is pouring into the ocean, carried by our

rivers. Nor do we help, for in our exploiting tactics we have removed tree and vegetation barriers which might anchor the soil
in place and prevent its being swirled away by winds or carried
down into the streams and rivers by excessive rain. To all this,
industry has added its quota by strip mining. With a total disregard
of nature, with an eye solely on profits, and with utter irrespon-
sibility for man's future needs, we have seen a technological rape of
our land. Top soil has been stripped and robbed of its fertility.
Vegetation has been destroyed—trees and plants. Chemical poisons
from the exposed mineral deposits have contaminated our streams
and killed the fish. The land has been left a virtual desert. Efforts
to control this are increasing, but we still have far to go.

Fourth, we have air pollution apart from the increase of the
carbon dioxide content.[24] Industry and automobiles are the chief
offenders, especially the latter. Internal combustion engines are
pouring carbon monoxide, hydrocarbons, and nitrogen oxides into
the atmosphere, incompletely combusted. Under the catalytic
action of the sunshine, a diversity of killing compounds are formed
out of these substances, including sulphuric acid with its effect on
human eyes and human clothing. Death-dealing carbon monoxide
and cancer-producing hydrocarbons also continue their work, while
the nitrogen oxides can be even more deadly. And when we add
the filthy smoke and chemical gases that industry is pouring into the
air to the pollution from the increasing number of automobiles, it
is not surprising that our great cities are covered by smog. Los
Angeles and San Francisco are outstanding examples, but the disease is common. Inefficient municipal incineration serves but to
multiply the problem. Not only man but the environment suffers.
In the Los Angeles Basin the smog has practically eliminated the
production of edible vegetables like spinach and lettuce, and it has
killed off many of the flowers. Citrus trees have been cut to half
their yield, and pine trees are being killed.

Fifth, we turn to the population burst.[25] The world's human
population is increasing at an alarming rate. The population of the
United States will reach 300 million by A.D. 2000. The possibilities
for the world by that year stagger the imagination when we remember that, in the undeveloped countries, about 40 percent of

the population are under 15 years of age and that they will produce offspring in the years immediately ahead. Modern medicine
and control of disease-bearing insects by pesticides have brought us
where we are. Now we must practice rigid birth control for the
survival of all. This problem is aggravated by narrow-minded and
short-sighted religionists whose eyes are presumably so fixed on the
hereafter that they have little realism in their attitudes to this
world.

The consequences of this tremendous population explosion have
only served to aggravate many of the problems already discussed.
The increased need for food will require self-sacrifice on the part
of the developed nations if the underdeveloped are not to starve.
It will need, as we have seen, a tremendous increase in the production of artificial fertilizers. But the red tide shows what these may
do to our oceans when they are carried into them by drainage from
the soil. William and Paul Paddock in a book entitled *Famine—
1975!* paint a gloomy picture. India and parts of South America
would seem to be heading for famine in the decade ahead. India's
population burst is far outstripping its food supply, and agricultural
development programs conjoined to birth control planning have
failed to keep up. The Paddocks suggest that if a nation shows no
signs of attaining self-sufficiency, the developed nations should
supply no further food from their own dwindling stocks. Rather,
they should concentrate on nations such as Pakistan which are
grimly struggling to self-sufficiency. Such a grim judgment finds
little support from a theologian. Yet it was an Anglican curate,
Malthus, who over a century ago saw famine, plague, and war as
the factors for eliminating a surplus population and preached the
survival of the fittest. This is no justification for refusing to listen
to a Christian conscience, but it may be a grim prediction of
realities in the days ahead.[26]

Again, the population increase will mean more automobiles and
more air pollution; more industrial production and great industrial
waste; more sewage and the danger of increased water pollution;
more garbage and a still greater problem of garbage disposal.

Sixth, the increased need for food, wood, and other natural
products means more need for pesticides, and immediately we face

the issue of DDT, already partly discussed. Persistent pesticides like DDT do not decompose quickly and remain to do much deadly work beyond their immediate objective. Rachel Carson's prophetic book, *The Silent Spring,* has been sadly vindicated. Graham's *Since Silent Spring* shows the entrenched nature of the pesticide industry and its continuing dissemination of false and distorted information. It demonstrates the reluctance of government agencies to act, and reports that though DDT is now increasingly banned, other virulent pesticides are still flowing into the world's markets. The organophosphates, already completely banned in Britain and the Soviet Union, are less persistent but more deadly. The mercury compounds are lethal, and Sweden has already banned them. We shall not know for years the fatal consequences of DDT in our oceans. It is so concentrated in the milk we drink that in our fatty tissues we Americans carry twelve parts to a million of DDT. Many birds are becoming extinct because of its effect—thin shells that prevent hatching of the embryo or fail to protect it. The National Audubon Society has reported the finding of one egg of the bald-headed eagle with no shell and simply protected by a membrane.

In the sea, DDT is affecting the photosynthesis of the algae, and thus upsetting the basic material in the food chain upon which fishes and our own sea food depend. The ecological pyramid is being sadly put out of balance. Actually, pesticides have done little for the increase of food production. Hal Borland[27] points out that the big increase in agricultural production took place before the use of the disputed pesticides. It was "due to intensified culture, new fertilizers, and, more important, better seed. Gains made since the advent of the chlorinated hydrocarbons are relatively small."

The presence of DDT affects genetic structures in organisms and may be a significant cause of cancer. At least, experiments on mice and rats show that this is true at the animal level, producing liver and lung tumors. The organophosphates can lead to serious consequences in the human nervous system. This is especially evident in migrant workers upon whom so often the task of spraying insecticides falls.

One special instance is the use of herbicides to defoliate the forests in Vietnam.[28] The chemicals used in the spraying contain concentrations ten times those recommended in the United States. They have also been used to destroy food crops. Many of them are cancer producing and cause birth abnormalities. Already birth abnormalities are reported to be on the increase in Vietnam. The effect on human beings and upon the eco-systems of the tropical world of Indo-China are likely to be disastrous. The potential productivity of the area may be so affected that it may be converted into a desert.

In the seventh place, we have the disposal of sewage and garbage. It is estimated that 1,500,000 gallons of raw sewage pass daily into Galveston Bay, and the effect on the shellfish industry of the area is massive. Increased population only multiplies the agony. Attempts to introduce sewage treatment and purification plants are making progress, but the problem of expense means that progress is often slow. The same problem of expense meets us in the case of garbage disposal. Incinerators increase the air pollution. Land fills are decreasing in availability. San Francisco has banned the contamination of its bay by this kind of disposal and is shipping its garbage to a desert area. New York has dumped its garbage in the ocean and now is realizing its effect upon the sea food of the area. What makes matters worse is the fact that some of our garbage, such as plastics, will not decompose. It all points to a simpler life and less technological devices to clutter up our world. But will modern man accept this?

Last in our catalogue, we must put the consequences of nuclear power. The effect of nuclear piles upon those who work in such power producers is still a matter of debate, however well protected such piles may be. At the moment, a bigger problem is the disposal of radioactive waste from such plants. We have been dumping it in the ocean along with like waste from hospitals and research institutions. Once more we are cutting our own throats by affecting our harvest from the sea. Wisdom is prevailing only a little, and the problem of safe disposal of deadly stuff still faces us.

POLITICAL EXPEDIENCY, INDUSTRIAL GREED, AND LIMITED PROGRESS

So much for the predatory activity of twentieth-century man. All is, of course, not dark. Efforts are being made by governments and responsible industrial leaders to deal with the situations. The scientists with troubled conscience have long been pleading for something to be done in the many areas involved. The villains are industrialists out for profits and technologists who apply scientific discovery to particular projects without considering the consequences. Then we have government bureaucracies which either drag their feet or quarrel among themselves. The question is whether the slow rate of progress is anywhere near sufficient to stem the tide of the advancing destruction of man and his planet.

Conservationists are banding together and fighting environmental exploitation in our law courts. Surprisingly, they are winning cases against those whose interest is solely economic gain. The courts are listening increasingly to those whose interest and responsibility are completely environmental and ruling against those with pecuniary concerns and clamant but purely selfish property rights. An outstanding example in America is the Sierra Club which has had its challenges of industrial exploitation upheld in several cases and has others pending. Now, concerned lawyers are seeking to fit environmental rights within the present law structure.

Scientists are, with increasing concern, trying to right the wrongs which technologists, agriculturalists, and industrialists have perpetrated in their application of scientific knowledge. We have already referred to the attempts to deal with the red tides off the Gulf and Californian coasts. Journals like the *Sierra Club Bulletin,* the *Audubon Magazine,* and others are devoting all their energies to the effects of pesticides upon bird life and fish life, to the imminent end of the whale at the hands of predatory man, to the continued destruction of our natural resources. Responsible journals, like *Saturday Review* and *The New Republic,* are increasingly concerned with ecological issues. The public is being challenged and taught by floods of paperbacks. And in every case, the core of such efforts is a group of responsible scientists who realize that their task is primarily to teach, not only within the university campus, but far beyond its confines.

Legislators at the state and federal levels continue to drag their feet. They can still be bought. The fear of losing votes is still a very significant factor in legislative bodies. Powerful corporations still lobby successfully with little concern for nature and with their eyes fixed on economic gain and greater profits. Yet let us note that, despite the dragging of feet across many years, DDT is banned, and in March of 1970 the White House of the United States promised action against other persistent pesticides by the end of the year. Other issues are not so bright, for people with the wrong sympathies still get into office. James Ridgeway[29] notes that the present "clean water team" in the United States government has landed itself in a muddle by making the "Mr. Clean Water" award to the president of the United States Steel Corporation. This concern is now threatened with legal proceedings by the government for being among the biggest water polluters in the nation! Ridgeway notes, too, that efforts to clean up the air have been confined by the Department of Health, Education, and Welfare to relatively small cities, while cities like Los Angeles and New York have so far not been called into consultation about clean air standards. His comment is significant: "It seems pretty clear that the laws aimed at pollution function to make it legitimate, providing a defensive cover for the chemical and energy industries which do most of the polluting, and at the same time encouraging the growth of competing technical staffs, whose livelihood in the simplest terms depends on continued environmental pollution."[30]

It is only fair to add at this point that New York is making a valiant effort to deal in a limited way with its problem.[31] A special task force appointed by Mayor Lindsay reported that the city would be uninhabitable within seven to ten years. Immediately, a responsible administration got to work. Consolidated Edison, a utility producer but also a major polluter, was constrained to use more clean-burning fuel. By this and other means the sulphur dioxide content of the air was reduced by 20 percent. Refuse incinerators were banned; garbage disposal methods were changed; the city reviewed its own contribution to the pollution problem through its various institutional buildings; high quality fuels were used for the city buses; demolition waste was no longer allowed to be burned. But the major problem still remains—the automobile. All cities are afflicted with its consequences. We need to install swift commuter

systems and eliminate the commuting automobile or else change
its motive power.

Another problem is the pollution of the air from major airports.
The jets project hydrocarbons into the atmosphere continuously
over New York and other major cities. As Cousins points out ". . .
the air at the airports, and especially in the vicinity of the runways,
is being saturated by poisons."[32]

The automobile and airplane industries are beginning to act responsibly. But the public needs also to act. It should examine its
own conscience in demanding high horsepower automobiles. Oil
companies are beginning to produce lead-free gasolines. Airplane
manufacturers are seeking ways of reducing the ejection of uncom-
busted hydrocarbons.

The public itself is being challenged at the political level by the
formation of the League of Conservation Voters.[33] This is a branch
of a group called Friends of the Earth. It plans actively to support
candidates with genuine ecological concern and to have representa-
tives and senators in the United States Congress who will not be
swayed by economic interests, industrial lobbying, and narrow political loyalties. Apart from this, the responsible electorate should exercise pressure on legislators at all levels—municipal, state, and federal.
Finally, a grave responsibility rests on the ordinary man.

Much of our discussion has turned on the American situation,
and rightly so. For we must clean out our own backyard if we
would give any leadership to our world. Yet the problem is world
wide. We have indicated many dimensions of this and also cited
individual countries which are striving to deal with it. We cannot
expect underdeveloped nations, with millions on the poverty line
and facing imminent famine, to have the ecological concern at all
levels. It is the developed nations that must provide the lead, and
this is becoming evident in pressures at the United Nations. Yet we
need more than the pressures in international politics. We need a
genuine concern for the welfare of all peoples. Immediately, the
religious dimension of ecology lifts its head, and especially the
Christian interpretation of this. Maybe we need to extend our
theological understanding of Christian mission, and to this we must
turn immediately.

There are, of course, gloomy prophets who believe there is no hope. There are cynics who point to the ultimate inevitability of the law of entropy with its promise of the heat-death of the universe. This is, however, a scientific myth, and its formulation assumes a closed block universe and grants no creative renewal to the future. There are humanists like Bloch and Garaudy who would deny this. Their recovery of an eschatological dimension is a growing challenge to Christian thinkers who know that God works and that the unexpected may be hidden in the veil of the future. This is not wishful thinking for the man of faith, but it does require that he participate in all ecological efforts to prepare the way for the coming of God. To the theological dimension we must now direct our attention.

FOUR

Contemporary Insights—
Philosophical and Theological

ANY SPECIFICALLY CHRISTIAN ATTEMPT to deal with the ecological problem needs a bridge to the corresponding attitude of the secular society in which the church finds itself. This means that any environmental theology needs to have an apologetic dimension in the sense of making its faith in God and its environmental concern intelligible to those who have a like concern but no accompanying theistic faith. We might describe this as one dimension of the new revolutionary attitude toward the future which is evident in both Christian and secular thought. The fact, already noted, that a theology of creation and a basic theistic humanism exist in biblical thought alongside the theology of redemption—the first expressed in the Wisdom Literature and the second brought to a focus in the prophetic workings—is a reminder that the roots of the Christian faith in its Hebrew tradition have a real concern for this world and for making the insights of faith relevant at the level of the "man in the street."

This business of building bridges to the secular mind is important in days when the old-style natural theology has to a large extent been jettisoned. The danger is that the Christian Church should make it appear that its environmental concern is just another attempt to ingratiate itself with the secular order by catching up with the latest "fad." We have to show that our concern at this point is a direct result of our faith and that we have something positive to contribute which is not available at the purely secular level. To do this we must make a theological interpretation of the ecological problem intelligible to those who do not share our faith-orientation, and this will mean starting where such people are. We cannot, of course, escape our faith presupposition, but fortunately the basic issue of the natural environment does provide a point of contact on which an acknowledged Christian theology of nature may be based. By this means we may at least begin to justify any specific Christian contribution that we have to offer to the debate on and motivation of any ecological crusade.

ECOLOGY AND THE PHILOSOPHY OF ORGANISM

Our investigation of the natural process has disclosed the wholeness and balanced interrelatedness in nature which may well be a pointer to some all-embracing and unifying principle. While no scientist would deny the element of probability and randomness in the scientific picture of the world, none would, at the same time, deny the ordered nature of the whole, however he might interpret this. There is a balance in nature upon which the modern ecological movement is building its hopes and its message, and this suggests some degree of meaningful patterning in which every member of an eco-system has its characteristic niche.

The contemporary renewal of interest in the thought of Alfred North Whitehead is suggestive at this point.[1] Whitehead argued that the scientific investigation of nature tended to carve nature up into discrete chunks of matter located and externally related in space and time. He described this as the "fallacy of misplaced concreteness" and argued that reality is not to be understood on the basis of such a mechanical model, but rather in terms of an organic model. He saw the world as an interrelated whole in which a vast array of "actual entities" were knit together by a network of "prehensions." By "actual entities" he meant the organic units which were constituent of the whole process, for nature is not composed of blocks of inert matter moving according to mechanical causation, but a complex of organisms. Even the so-called inanimate or purely physical order is actually organic. By "prehensions," Whitehead meant that such unitary organisms were related to one another by rudimentary feelings. The latter were at various levels of unconsciousness and consciousness, depending upon the status of the particular actual entity. Thus each actual entity was feelingfully related to other actual entities. Furthermore, it not only prehended these but also prehended the "subjective aim" by which its own particular role was prescribed.

Whitehead would thus picture reality as a process in which the universe as a whole embraces a vast nexus of actual entities related to each other by various degrees of feeling or prehension. He regarded the dichotomy of mind from matter as a false and artificial abstraction. All actual entities of the universe must be pictured in organic terms with the sensitivity and interrelatedness discoverable at the level of living organisms. In addition, they must be thought of on this basis as dipolar. They each possess both a physical and a mental pole. By the latter, they prehend their particular subjective aim, their place and function within the process as a whole. By the former, they prehend other actual entities in relation to which their own subjective aim must be "satisfied." The idea of satisfaction brings in a time factor, for no actual entity can be prehended by any other until it has attained satisfaction, fulfilled its subjective aim. Once that has happened, it attains objectivity and perishes. It persists only as it is prehended by other actual entities which seek satisfaction of their own subjective aims in relation to it and to all other actual entities which have, in like manner, attained satisfaction. This emphasis on time means that prehensions by the physical pole are always of what has already become and not of what is in process of becoming. Whitehead's comprehension of relativity made him avoid contemporaneity at this level.

This approach to reality has peculiar significance when we remember what we have already noted both in the biblical view of nature and in the biological study of eco-systems. The kind of interrelatedness that Whitehead envisages does give expression to truths which are expressed in differing ways in both.

What then is the theological import of such an approach? Has it theistic implications? Whitehead would see the whole process as a manifestation of creativity and uses the latter as an all-embracing descriptive category. Thus the process is itself a creative one within which the new and unexpected may emerge. But the wholeness and organic interrelatedness of the whole point to the need for deity, even though the latter is not given the absolute creative role ascribed by Christian thinking. For the unity and wholeness of the process in which each actual entity fulfills its role and fills what ecologists would call its niche requires an ordering principle. So Whitehead argues that the subjective aims, evident in the various constituent members of the process, are chosen and given them by God, who is himself the prime manifestation of creativity. The deity selects these subjective aims from the "eternal objects," akin to Plato's ideas, which in some sense subsist in reality. These are contemplated by God and dealt with aesthetically. So God is the reality who provides aesthetic order to the whole. God does not create the process, but he directs it. Whitehead's approach is, however, fundamentally organic and aesthetic rather than personal and moral.

Discussing, as we are, the ecological issue, such an organic model for the universe is both attractive and relevant, yet it does not give an adequate understanding of personal being. We shall turn shortly to a discussion of the issue of personal self-transcendence as this is now being raised by Marxist humanists. The capacity of man to transcend the natural process of which he is a part and in which he is involved, so that he is able to direct and control it to some degree, has already been considered. But just at this level of self-transcendence, Whitehead's approach becomes unsatisfactory. Since he regards all actual entities as momentary, attaining satisfaction and objectivity and then perishing only to persist in their objective immortality, he has real difficulty in dealing adequately with personal identity. For persons become a succession, a temporal nexus, of momentary organisms, and their enduring character depends upon prehensions in forms of memory and anticipation. "I" persist as an identity in the light of the memory of previous momentary selves, and the present self attains satisfaction in its prehension of such past actual occasions. The absence of any persistent "I-ness" which both transcends the personal process and is immanent throughout it, knitting it together, raises real issues for the understanding of personal being. Furthermore, self-transcendence cannot find a satisfactory explanation if we employ a model from the lower level of organism.

It is here that Whitehead's conception of God raises difficulties. For he defines God as an actual entity and as himself in process. He also is dipolar, possessing both a mental and a physical pole. The mental pole constitutes God's primordial nature in which he envisages the eternal objects and selects the subjective aims for the other actual entities in the world-process. He thus is the "principal of concretion," providing the aesthetic order for the organismic whole, and doing this continuously as arrays of actual entities successively attain satisfaction and objective immortality. But he has also a physical pole in which he prehends all the actual entities involved in the process. This pole constitutes God's consequent nature, whereby he accompanies the process which he directs, is enriched by it, and suffers with it. God can thus be described as the fellow traveler of the world, involved in the world's process of becoming, and moving from his primordial to his consequent nature as he enjoys the movement of the world. But if God is an actual entity, he should also be a nexus of successive satisfactions, and his enduring character should, like that of other actual entities, be subject to the same temporal prehensions of memory and anticipation. Here Whitehead stops short, for he thinks of God as an enduring actual entity, presiding over and directing the process in all its temporal dimensions. Once more the inadequacy of the organic model becomes evident. Whitehead has sought, in the case of deity, to return to some sense of enduring being, and revealed the Achilles heel of his system. He recognizes that, in some very real sense, the world-process is incorporated in and contributes to the divine life, but a better understanding of personal being would have made Whitehead's thought more consistent.

What is important, however, is Whitehead's recognition that the authentic balance of the universe might well point to some kind of deity. His is a much more tentative advocacy of the teleological argument. The chief difficulty lies as always with the issue of imbalance in the process, the presence of the dysteleological elements, the mystery of evil in all its forms. On this, any natural theology tends to shipwreck, and Whitehead fails to deal adequately with the issue. He retains an open-ended universe and emphasizes its creativity, the continuing possibility of emergent novelty. Yet he always ties up the roles of the actual entities with the selection of such subjective aims by God, and thereby can provide no adequate rationale for the presence and operation of evil.

Contemporary process-thinking at the theological level is liable to the same weaknesses. These are the struggles to find an adequate understanding of the personal on the basis of the organic model, and the difficulty of dealing with the issues raised by natural and moral evil when the emphasis falls upon an aesthetic order presumably adequately provided by the deity. Yet the insight remains. The basis of this metaphysical thinking is very evident in the ecological aspects of the actual process. A more realistic recognition that no eco-system is in perfect balance, that natural evil and contingency are very present, would vitiate any attempt at a rigidly logical development, but the presence of balance and interrelatedness may well point to an ordering presence. Furthermore, Whitehead's organic model and the attempts of his followers to build panpsychic systems for the universe would suggest that we need to reassess the nature of matter and to ask whether there is such a kinship between matter and mind that mind is able to understand and control this physical order. Finally, the reality of eco-systems might well suggest that attempts to explain these in terms of purely mechanical relationships may be abstractions from an interrelatedness which has much richer dimensions. The latter may require something of that internal nexus of relationships which Whitehead sought to define by his term "prehension."

THEISTIC POINTERS—MARXIST HUMANISM AND MAN ON HIS OWN

The pointers provided by ecological balance are not the sole basis for a theistic orientation. We need to turn to the evolutionary process as a whole within which such eco-systems have developed. It has already been noted that the process would appear to be a directed process in the sense that it leads to the emergence of man, self-transcendent personal being with the capacity to appraise absolute values. In man the process has become self-conscious, and with human freedom it has the power to control itself in the light of the response to the vision of truth, beauty, and goodness. We have already developed this thesis and attacked the idea that such values are the product of the process itself and thus evolutionary adaptations. Rather, we have argued that their presence precipitates a crisis when man appears within the balanced eco-system and refuses to use his freedom aright. We are now becoming increasingly aware of this crisis in the process. Words like "sin," "alienation," "estrangement," "demonic" are gaining much more significance now that the ecological issue has been conjoined to the issues raised by war, poverty, and race. Nor can humanistic optimism provide a sufficient answer to the problems that beset contemporary man. This is becoming evident in the current Marxist/Christian dialogue.[3]

Following upon the thought of the earlier Marx, thinkers like Garaudy and Bloch are sponsoring a humanistic version of the Marxist philosophy. This rejects the full-blooded materialistic determinism of orthodox Marxism and sees man as in some sense a creative agent within the complex of economic forces. Garaudy has shown that the deterministic interpretation of history and its understanding of man as subject to necessary and inevitable forces is not a fair interpretation of Marx.[4] Marx did see man as a creative center but held that, to be a significant factor in history, man must understand the forces which were dynamically operative in social change. Yet Marx did not make any serious attempt to understand man himself, and at this point the newer Marxist humanists are prepared to learn from Christianity. They no longer dismiss religion as an opiate of the people but recognize that it can be and has been a creative factor in the movement of man's social life. They believe that this has its roots in the eschatological dimension of the Hebrew/Christian tradition and point out that this futuristic reference has been preserved in their own philosophical approach to reality. They do recognize, however, that in the Christian faith there is an understanding of transcendence which they themselves lack.

This understanding has two points of reference—at the level of the structure of personal being with the emphasis on self-transcendence, and at the theistic level with the emphasis on divine transcendence. With regard to the first point of reference, such Marxists acknowledge their deficiency in the understanding of personal subjectivity. For the Christian, man's self-transcendence enables him to rise above the process and makes creative freedom and historical decision possible. Here the Marxist sees matter for dialogue, in the light of his newly awakened concern for man's initiative in social revolution. Thus we find Bloch stressing the forward movement of reality in which an unfinished past is moving forward to a yet open future. He sees the present as the "front" at which men experience the "not yet," something which may become actual by their decisive action. Furthermore, the future is open so that the "not yet" contains the possibility of the new, the *novum*. Mankind is ever moving forward to its "homeland," its Utopia, and the movement of history is activated by a "principle of hope." The category of "not-yet-being" contains the promise of the future. It describes the way in which the future exercises a creative influence upon man's present struggle to realize himself in relation to his world. The "not-yet" is the future that makes men free. Harvey Cox writes that "Man is not, for Bloch, principally a product of his past either individually or as a race. Man is not to be described as 'thinker' or 'symbol maker' or 'tool maker' or even as 'worker.' Man is the 'hope-er', he who-hopes. His essential existence tip-toes along the narrow ridge between the disappearing 'now' and the ever newly appearing 'not yet.' And his basic stance, when he is true to himself, is that of creative expectation, a hope that engenders action in the present to shape the future."[5]

What we miss with Bloch is any concern with absolute values in the facing of the future, for Bloch remains an uncomfortable atheist. Once again we face the issue of transcendence. In the Christian tradition, divine transcendence carries both the sense of the contrast of the perfect with the imperfect, the eternal with the transcendent, the immutable with the mutable, the Creator with the

created, being with becoming, and the sense of the contrast between
the divinely planned future and the human present with its limita-
tions and frustrations. It has been pointed out that the former leads
to a contemplative and the latter to an active form of human existence.[6] The latter also brings in the eschatological dimension
whereas the former emphasizes those absolute values without which
Christian activism could not function.

Bloch's humanism finds no sure footing once the divine dimension of transcendence in reality is ignored. His emphasis on the future provides him with the only transcendent dimension which can
give sanction to his position, and he reinforces this by his view of
"matter." He does not regard "matter" in a materialistic sense
since he views it as containing the potential for the whole movement of nature and history. Rather like Alexander's space/time,[7]
it is endowed with future developments and would seem to possess
a nisus or drive toward the future with all its novelties, including
man and his creative freedom. Matter is no longer understood in
materialistic terms. Rather it has become the matrix from which
life, mind, spirit emerge. It becomes a dynamic and creative stuff,
an inexhaustible ground for all future novelties. Thus there are
many who would describe Bloch as a crypto-theist, for he is ascribing to "matter" many of the qualities which the theist finds in the
deity. Thus Moltmann contends that "the transcendence of the
creator is made immanent in the matter of creation. This de-
mythologization is seen as necessary to an activation of human hope.
In reality, the result is a remythologization of nature. . . ."[8] Human
hopes are now attached to the possibilities inherent in nature, and
we have a "humanizing of nature" and a "naturalizing of man."

As for transcendence, Bloch sees this sensible universe as the sum
total of reality. Yet he also believes that man's ideational structures
may cause significant changes in the historical process. He thus
sees the significance of values in history without finding their roots
in the physical order. Presumably they too arise out of the potential
and creative dynamism of "matter." Man is left with the courage
of hope and that is all. Such courage may be thwarted. Man's ideational structures may not conquer, but he must courageously take

his plunge, succeed or fail. The future is completely open, and there is no transcendent backing to man's values.

Finally, Bloch takes his stand on the future, the realm of new possibilities, as the transcendent reference of historical existence. It is this future which lures man on to creative activity. Both Bloch and Garaudy dismiss any idea of God as a world-ruler. Garaudy argues that the very name of God must be rejected because the name implies a presence, a reality, a necessary being, which answers to the inadequacy of our relative and partial being.[9] Such a reality, Bloch contends, would deny our human freedom and close the openness of the future. Christians are right in their eschatological emphasis but wrong in filling the future with God. Man must be sensitive to the transcendence of the future with all its possibilities for novelty in the historical process. There is a "homeland," and we need an eschatological openness in which there is a passionate concern for the coming of freedom. For such thinkers, "God" means a closed future and the ultimate demolition of freedom.

Bloch finds that the field of religious hypostases postulated in the idea of the Kingdom of God is more lasting than the hypostases themselves. But now everything turns on man. The pressure of the "not yet" implies *"an open effective sphere* for the human subject, as well as for a far from finished subject of the natural environment."[10] Yet here chaos and Kingdom hang in the balance, and "it is human achievement in history that will weigh down the scale of nothingness or that of all."[11] Thus for such Marxist humanists the one and only goal of all religious history has been "the realm of lifting the *incognito* of human and mundane depth."[12] They live "a never satisfied exigency of totality and absoluteness, of omnipotence as to nature and of perfect loving reciprocity of consciousness."[13] This exigency, this transcendence, is completely open and bound up with man's achievement. The principle of hope has no *sure* ground in such transcendence, but the courageous expression of it may yet lead to that homeland of freedom for which man hopes. Ahead there is a vacuum which must be kept open "for a possible, still undecided reality of the future."[14]

Hence, Bloch calls for wonder. He believes that the religious category of miracle contains a truth. The truth lies in the concept of leap, for nature does make leaps—"the world moves in leaps (by means of history) and permits breakthroughs (without any transcendent alliances or interventions)."[15] This is supported by the dialectical basis of Marx's thought. What this new humanism calls for is a concrete utopianism which springs out of a dialectical process. Each lived moment is *incognito* and calls for a "hopeful faith in something *substantially still undetermined* but *unmistakably wonderful.*"[16] This is not superstition but a part of the dialectical process in which "matter" and man himself are involved. Man must face the inconclusive future with a belief in wonder that is hopeful but "it implies no statement referring, or capable of referring, to anything other than hints, presemblances, pre-experiences, or cyphers in the existing, objectively real world."[17]

We have spent much time on this new humanism because it does offer a real option in the facing of the ecological issue. It has no final and certain rooting in transcendence; it places man in the center and really builds upon its understanding of a dynamic "matter" in dialectical process towards an open future; it therefore sees the future as all or nothing, as order or chaos. Yet it does call for hope because that future is inconclusive; for a belief in wonder, the *novum* that may emerge at any moment as man uses his creative freedom; for an expectation that excludes mechanistic determinism. Can it equally exclude God? A deistic *ex machina* who intervenes in the process? Yes! But a transcendent presence who embraces the whole process, who is immanently active within it, and who in love is guiding it to an ultimate consummation in which creativity and freedom shall be fully expressed? No!

We must note that the Marxist humanists are concerned with nature as much as with man. Since their future concerns the whole process, and since man's creative activity is directed solely on and within the process, they see the "not yet" as inclusive. Man and his environment together move forward creatively into the inconclusive and open future which ever lures them on. The Marxist emphasis on transcendence as the future needs to be matched by an emphasis on the transcendence of absolute values. It is difficult to see a deep motivation for the transformation of nature and the restoration of its balance, unless there is some sense of moral responsibility to what transcends man.

A humanistic motivation would generally be concerned for the preservation of the human race and not involve any deeper responsibility for nature. The very fact that the whole process is a directed one might suggest that it has a greater significance than just that of providing an environment for its supreme emergent, man. The fact that man is activated by a desire for values which often transcend and even cut across his own desires is a reminder that human self-transcendence needs a component self-transcendence in the universe if such values are to be intelligible. It points to a personal transcendence in the process as a whole akin to that without which the emphasis on man's creativity and freedom cannot really be understood. The recognition of a need for personal self-transcendence at the human level, if man is to be other than a pawn of material forces, might suggest that this could provide a model for understanding the world-process as a whole. Granted such a transcendent presence, man's concern for his environment gains a deeper significance than that of his own self-preservation. It may be bound up with a purpose in which nature as well as man plays an abiding part. The search for truth, beauty, and moral worth may then be concerned not just with man himself, but also with the material process in which man is involved and out of which he has emerged. Nature too may be mourning a lost good.

This would certainly make the emphasis on the future more intelligible. It is difficult to see how an eschatology grounded in absence rather than presence can finally encourage hope and wonder, yet such would be necessary for the ecological enterprise. Nor does the emphasis on "matter" as dynamic and creative provide a sufficient ground for that self-transcendence in man without which human creative directness cannot function. If we describe such "matter" in pantheistic terms and speak of a growing God, ultimately such a God cannot be less than the creatures in which his life is manifested.

Enough has been said to indicate, we hope, that a theistic option might be suggested by the very process into which man finds himself thrown.

The Theological Concern with Process
and the Secular

The impact of science upon twentieth-century thought and life has had its theological repercussions. Increasingly, not merely at the ecological level but in every approach of man to his world, theoretical and practical, it has led often to revolutionary transformations in thought and behavior. Since the Enlightenment, theologians have directed their attention more and more upon the process of nature and history, recognizing that nature is also a historical development as the evolutionary viewpoint has made evident and that the Christian faith is so tied to a historical disclosure that a searching estimate of historical knowledge is necessary. The theologians of the last century, from Schleiermacher to Troeltsch, were all preoccupied with these issues and were asking questions which we are now asking once more. Between them and us there stands Karl Barth with his thundering attempt to put a quietus on all questioning and to put ourselves under the downward striking Word of God. Tillich did, however, sustain a bridge between the pre-Barthian thinkers and ourselves, while Bonhoeffer began to ask the questions again and to confront man with a world that was dominated by the results of science and technology.

Increasingly in the last two decades, theologians have become concerned with this world process, with the secular, its historical movement, and its changing natural environment. As a result, we have seen secular concerns moving to the forefront of theological thought and serious attempts to deal with the burgeoning knowledge with which scientific and historical investigations and thinking now confront us. Out of this ferment, three significant lines of thought have emerged—process thinkers like Daniel Day Williams, Norman Pittenger, Richard Overman, John B. Cobb, Jr., and Charles Hartshorne; creative evolutionary thinkers in the school of Teilhard de Chardin; and the theologians of hope with their emphasis on the future, such as Wolfhart Pannenberg, Jürgen Moltmann, Johannes Metz, and Edward Schillebeeckx. Because all these thinkers are very much concerned with this world-process and have insights into the creative dimensions and divine significance of the natural order, we shall pass them briefly in review.

We have already made a passing reference to process theology in discussing the thought of Alfred North Whitehead. Building upon the latter, such thinkers[18] have constructed a panpsychic model of the universe in which the idea of organism is basic. They labor with the problem of the nature of the personal, especially when they lean too closely on Whitehead. However, they offer many insights which should enrich theological thought and which do not belong solely to their approach. We can only offer some of these basic insights, since to review each of the thinkers in turn would occupy too much space. The universe is pictured in panpsychic terms and regarded as bound together by feeling, which finds its supreme expression in love and which is brought to a focal point in the love of God. Leaving a place for complete individuality and freedom in the universe, these thinkers find in love the cement which holds it together and the force which gives it direction as a process. For they are convinced that, as befits their organic model, the universe is a moving and creative process within which the new and unexpected may occur.

In varying degrees of dependence upon Whitehead's scheme of thought, the world is envisaged in panpsychic terms. It is constituted of a vast aggregate of psychic entities, organismic units with various levels of consciousness or sensitivity and in diverse degrees of interrelationship. Thus, some may be aggregated into larger groupings like a pile of sand, which can be described as a democratic society with all the members at the same level of relationship. Others may be built together into larger organismic groupings like the human being. They can be described as monarchical societies. Thus, in man, the soul is the focal and dominant psychic entity, with other entities related to it at varying levels of interrelatedness and constituting thereby the human body. In this way, thinkers like Hartshorne can describe the universe as an organic whole in which every constituent part is related and sensitive to all other parts. The whole universe as such is in creative process, and within it novelty may at any time emerge.

The latter is possible because we have no haphazard movement but an orderly development in which the central factor is the divine reality. The process thinkers describe their thought as panentheistic, intending thereby to rule out both a deism which so emphasizes the divine transcendence that God becomes an "absentee deity" and also a pantheism which identifies God with the world. They think of God as the all-embracing reality who contains the universe within his own life, and thus is both immanent in and transcendent to the world. We have always sought to narrow panentheism to a view which rejects *creatio ex nihilo,* absolute creation out of nothing and regards the world as issuing from the divine "stuff." We prefer to retain the description "theism" for the traditional Christian understanding which postulates absolute creation while retaining both the divine transcendence and immanence. In this sense, most process thinkers are panentheistic in the narrow sense. They regard the world as organic to God's own life and incorporated totally within that life. The creatures are related and sensitive to God, each in its own characteristic way, and God is related and sensitive to them.

Hartshorne can describe God's action on his creatures as "persuasion," and he allows for the fact that the universe is so created that limits are set to the freedom of the creatures. God sets an optimum of conditions for the freedom of all beings, so that there is a balance between undue risk and overmuch security, both of which would be too costly for freedom.[19] Daniel Day Williams argues that the characteristics of human love must have "their analogues in the being of God" if God is love and "the ground of the structure of love."[20] He defines the characteristic categories of love as "individuality and communion with the other, freedom, action, and suffering, causality which leaves the other free to be moved by the other, and impartiality of judgment." Following his reasoning, he then, as do all other process thinkers, attacks the idea of God as immutable. God is not nontemporal in all respects, but rather the human characteristics of love are exemplified in his own being. He is involved with his creatures, and they enrich his life as they play their part in his experience. Although Williams is concerned especially with the level of human experience, his understanding of divine love undergirds his whole approach to the created order.

Hartshorne describes God in Whiteheadian terms as dipolar,

both being and becoming. The process is organic to the divine life, so that God himself is enriched by the development within the created order. Thus he thinks even of the divine perfection in dynamic terms. At every stage of the process, God is the norm of perfection, but it is a norm in process. Hartshorne can speak therefore of the "divine relativity" in the sense of God's active involvement with and relativity to his world. Such relativity means that God's being as love is enriched as that love is both operative in and responded to by his world. Furthermore, as the creatures relate to one another, that relationship is also integral to the divine experience of becoming. God enjoys his world and suffers with it, so that both enrichment and suffering can be predicated of him. Indeed, Pittenger contends that the world is not "adjectival to God in the sense that what happens in it is expressive of, but without real effect upon, the divine reality."[22]

Again, God's relation to his world is thought of in terms of immanence and transcendence. The world is in God, and God is present throughout his universe. Only so can the world-process be an integral part of his experience. But Hartshorne's description of God as dipolar, as both being and becoming, points to an inner essential core of the divine life, God's love which finds expression in his relativity. It is in this way that transcendence must be understood. God is not exhausted by his presence and operation in the created order. His transcendence is likened to saying that a man transcends and is not exhausted by his action.[23] Elsewhere, Pittenger uses the model of personal depth,[24] and thus approaches the analogy of personal self-transcendence. Just as we are *in* our work yet *more than* our work, so God operates in the world without being lost in the operation. ". . . he is the unexhausted and inexhaustible Reality who works through all things yet ever remains himself."[25] From his inexhaustible depths, he is ever energizing both in nature and in history and fulfilling his purpose in it.

Such a view, process thinkers contend, obviates the language of intervention and inbreak, so often used in theologies which have deistic tendencies. In this kind of thinking there is no need to postulate a "God of the gaps," as if the divine activity were an intrusion into the normal world-processes. God pervades every part of and movement in the world by his presence and energizing activity.

Yet he does so in a way that preserves the freedom of the creatures and the relative independence of the created order. This holds because God is supreme love, a love so supreme that even the most radical freedom cannot defeat it. This holds at every level of the process, the natural order as well as the realm of human history. Pittenger holds that "we may say that God is love because he is infinitely related; he is love because he enters into and participates in his creation; he is love, supremely, because he absorbs error, maladjustment, evil, everything that is ugly and unharmonious, and is able to bring about genuine and novel occasions of goodness by the use of material which seems so unpromising and hopeless."[26] God is no dictator. He has concern for the created order at all levels. He works in and through the created occasions of his world, energizing, eliciting response, lovingly persuading, and providing data for the new occasions as they arise.[27] At the human level, above all, this supremely self-giving and persuasive love operates amid the conflict of finite wills and the confusion of historical events to accomplish its purpose.

In such understanding of the process, theologians like Williams and Pittenger would make the Incarnation central, yet in a way consistent with their panentheistic stance. We find Pittenger emphasizing the humanity of Jesus. Jesus was genuine man in whom there was increasing moral and spiritual discernment, obedience to the divine will, and employment for the divine purpose as he responded "to the movement of the divine activity, the Word, in him."[28] As man, his response was full and entire so that he became the unique instrument of God, the incarnation of the Word. On the divine side, the divine presence and activity everywhere in the process provides the background for that unique divine energizing whereby Jesus of Nazareth was the Word Incarnate. In the Cross we thus have a unique disclosure of that redemptive suffering with which God continually in love accompanies the process of his universe. It is by such an alchemy of love that God wills to transmute evil and human wickedness into good. Furthermore, in that redemptive and suffering love, men are being summoned to cooperate with God in the completion of his world-process.

How does eschatology fit into this approach? There is always the possibility of the emergence of novelty, and the universe is open ended. It is an ongoing process, and process thinkers seem to feel that God without such a process would cease to be what he discloses himself to be. Pittenger can write: "So far as we know, there is no 'ending' of the movement. It is everlasting in the sense of a continuous and unceasing development, on the whole moving towards fuller realization of heterogeneous yet organically inter-related goods, even though there is 'evil' with maladjustments, 'backwaters,' and elected failure to advance at many points along the line."[29] Hence, he can speak of God as eternal in his being and everlasting in his becomingness. Yet, when the same thinker concerns himself with the Incarnation, he more explicitly speaks of God's ultimate ruling as the Reality who is love and light and truth. Even here, however, no temporal end is envisaged, but rather we are reminded of "the Kingdom of God which abides for ever."[30]

The ongoing process is to be understood theologically in terms of the Incarnation. Here Pittenger makes a valuable contribution parallel to that of Teilhard de Chardin which we shall discuss subsequently. He, more than most process thinkers, endeavors to preserve an incarnational theology. His understanding of the Incarnation sets the unique event of Jesus Christ within a general setting of divine immanence. God is everywhere energizing in his world, and his energizing in Jesus of Nazareth is a unique manifestation whereby Jesus is the Word Incarnate. Hence the Incarnation becomes a kind of "template" for the whole process. God is actively operating within the created order until the whole "becomes, in some sense, 'the body of God.' "[31] He is working in and energizing through the process over which his love is supremely regnant. Thus at the different levels of the created order he is present and operative in a way appropriate to that level. His presence in living matter will be at a different degree of intensity from his presence in human history. But living things and historical movements alike are media of his self-expression. Jesus as the Word Incarnate is the supreme manifestation of what God is doing throughout the process. In varying degrees, with all heights of attainment and depths of failure that human freedom and the quasi-independence of the natural order involve, God is incarnating himself in the world-process, winning his way by the persuasion of his supreme love, energizing in the world at all levels. Thus Pittenger would see the whole process as a movement to incarnation, although he would recognize that the intensity of the incarnational indwelling varies with the particular levels of the process. In the Incarnation, God shows us what he is about. The Incarnation is "an action which shows the meaning of it all."[32]

This theological approach has much to commend it. It is hopeful about nature and history and is very concerned with this world. It sees the world-process as an unfinished one in which men are summoned to cooperate with God and assist in the fulfillment of the divine purpose. Furthermore, because the world is not a finished product and because God is immanent, energizing in it, the unexpected and the novel may appear. Again, God in his supreme love is dealing with the evil, the creaturely errors, the arrogance of his creatures at all levels, operating always for the fulfillment of his purpose. His inexhaustible reservoirs of love give the ground for hope and call on man to work within God's purpose at the levels of both nature and history. For God's purpose involves the whole.

This kind of theology recognizes the organic interrelatedness of man and nature. The Christian should have a moral concern for nature. It is not *just* a background for man and his history, significant as the latter may be. Nature itself is also an historical process moving from the primordial chaos in evolutionary development. It too has a history, as the Genesis 1 story of creation attempts to express. It too is moving towards a consummation which the biblical writers could describe as "a new heaven and a new earth." It has its part to play in the divine purpose, and the task of cooperating with God in the process has ecological perspectives as well as those belonging to man's spiritual, social, and cultural life. This approach would be expected in the light of the basic philosophy of organism upon which this type of theology is based.

EVOLUTION AND CHRISTIFICATION

We turn now to the insights of Teilhard de Chardin[33] whose posthumous works have stimulated many contemporary thinkers and about whose thought a vast collection of volumes has appeared. The fact that Julian Huxley wrote a foreword to *The Phenomenon of Man* shows that Teilhard's interpretation of the evolutionary process has an attraction for those who adopt a naturalistic stance.

Teilhard was himself an anthropologist of repute as well as a trained Jesuit priest. He writes as a scientist but also with theological understanding. He belongs to a group of thinkers—Lloyd Morgan, Samuel Alexander, Henri Bergson, Jan Smuts, William Temple—who were convinced that the scientific evidence for evolution had to be incorporated basically into any philosophical system. Hence, he makes the evolutionary model basic in his understanding of the world process. Yet while he builds upon the evidence of the sciences, he acknowledges that his initial approach goes beyond science. He argues that the process of evolution cannot be fully understood without taking account of man himself, the more so because it is in and through man that the process has become self-conscious, so that its processes and mechanisms can be comprehended and even controlled. Once man is included, with all the varied responses of which he is capable, the process of evolution discloses aspects with which the physical and even the biological sciences are not adequate to deal. Man has an inner side to his nature and his mental characteristics must, in some way, be reflected in the process from which he has emerged.

With this kind of approach Teilhard finds a basic law of complexification/interiorization working throughout evolutionary development. By this he means that at every level there is an inner as well as an outer aspect to the process and that, as the process develops higher levels with increasing complexity of organization, there is also a deepening of its inner dimension. This interiorization is seen as the physical order reaches a complexity of structure sufficient for life to emerge and for a skin of life, a biosphere, to be spread around the earth. Life manifests an interior aspect, for living things operate as wholes from increasing inner depths of consciousness and sensitivity. As life moves upward, this interior aspect is centralized increasingly in the cerebrum. When the nervous system has attained sufficient centralization in the process of cerebralization, man emerges and consciousness moves to self-consciousness.

Now a skin of mind, a noosphere, is spread around the planet, and the process of evolution becomes self-conscious, able to direct itself.

Teilhard refuses any attempt at reductionism, to explain the higher in terms of the lower and to reduce mind and life to the level of mechanistic action which characterizes the physical level of reality. Rather, he holds that the energy which is the basic stuff from which the process took its rise is not purely physical. It has two dimensions or components, a physical and a mental, a without and a within, a tangential and a radial. At the physical level, the tangential component is central and is responsible for the increasing aggregation of the energy into the complex molecules which are the basis of life. At a certain point in history, these complex structures had reached a stage when the process became supersaturated. The outward structures folded back upon themselves and the inner or radial component of energy began to make itself evident. The tangential component still pointed the way to increasing complexity of structures as living organisms proceeded with the centralization of the controlling nervous system and the development of the cerebrum. In all this, the radial component became increasingly significant until, in an area somewhere between the Odulvai Gorge and Java, the process again became supersaturated and folded back upon itself. Now there emerged man, and the radial component of energy came to fuller flower.

At this point, Teilhard looks for directiveness. Like the process theologians, he finds the key in love. As the process becomes self-directed with the emergence of man, it faces two possibilities— either it may move back to the totalitarian anthill or forward to new social possibilities in which men find their true freedom in a relationship of love. Evolution has now ceased at the physical and almost at the biological levels. It is in the skin of the noosphere that it is now proceeding, and with its direction human decisions are intimately concerned. Teilhard believes that the pressures of the population burst and other factors in the human environment are forcing decisions which may lead in one of the two ways just mentioned. But he contends that ultimately freedom in love must take over and the process move towards its next point of supersaturation when the hyperpersonal will emerge. This hyperpersonal does not mean the loss of the personal but rather the building together of personal beings into a complex of relationships activated by love and concern. In such a setting, persons will not lose their freedom but rather find their true freedom as they commit themselves to the life and well-being of the whole. Already we can see Teilhard's Christian convictions breaking through his reasoning.

Now if this directiveness to the hyperpersonal is to be possible, it means that the process is directed towards what Teilhard calls Point Omega, and this Point Omega will be characterized by certain qualities. It will be a controlling point or final cause which lures the whole process onwards—how Thomistic! It attracts and moves the evolutionary movement forward. To be effective, such a Point Omega must be both loving and lovable; personal, if it is to effect a personal union of beings in a higher whole; transcendent, if it is not to succumb to the Second Law of Thermodynamics which is regnant in the world process; and present as well as future, if it is truly to influence the current existents in the process. This Point Omega is identified by Teilhard with God!

There we have an attempt to think of the divine transcendence in terms of a temporal model as future. God is the absolute and all-embracing future. As Teilhard turns to his Christian faith, implicit through all his thought but, at this juncture, becoming explicit, he sees this divine future becoming present in Jesus Christ and the Incarnation. Thereby the process is redirected from within. The Incarnation initiates a process of Christification in which the whole universe will be incorporated in Christ—a very strong resemblance here to the process theology of thinkers like Pittenger. In the Church the hyperpersonal is already being realized proleptically. Teilhard offers us a Christology in which the humanity of our Lord is an incorporating humanity.

He also seems to offer us a cosmic eschatology in which the redemption of the individual is seen within the setting of social and cosmic redemption. There is considerable debate here, since Teilhard does not unambiguously state his position. He clearly identifies the attainment of the hyperpersonal, as human society involutes around Omega Point, with the Second Advent. He uses apocalyptic language quite often at this juncture. He seems to think of the ultimate consummation as the ecstatic communion of the saints pictured in Catholic thought as the pulsating mystic rose. Does he then envisage the whole cosmos as participating in the ultimate redemption or only personal beings with their historical achievements? He certainly takes the Second Law of Thermodynamics seriously, as in his discussion of Omega Point. Does he think, however, of an apocalyptic transformation which embraces the whole, even the biological and the physical? He evidently does not think of the end as a natural outcome of the process. We need to remember that he does not regard the mechanisms of biological evolution as operative at the human level. With the emergence of man, human freedom, human hates and human loves, human decisions and human creativeness came into play. He does not regard the attainment of Omega Point as inevitable from the logical point of view, since he recognizes the reality of sin and evil, perhaps not always as much as he ought. He believes, however, that the general trend of the process is in this direction, and he reinforces this with his faith. For the attainment of Omega Point is not just natural but spirit directed. "The universe," he tells us, "is heating up, is opening itself to the forces of love."[34] Man is no longer the spectator of evolution, but its creative subject, and spiritual forces are luring him on. Thus when Omega Point is attained, it will be because the spiritual has been operating within the natural. The Christ is at work. However temporally distant it may be, there are signs of the End. Humanization is now pointing to Christification. The Second Law of Thermodynamics must be matched by the population burst. "Pressed tightly against one another by the increase in their numbers and relationship, forced together by the growth of a common power and the sense of a common travail, the men of the future will in some sort form a single consciousness."[35] There will then, face to face with God, be a truly human decision, a "turning inward" of consciousness, an eruption of interior life, an ecstasy. The interiorization will be complete. The Parousia will occur!

What then of the tangential component of energy? Will it be shed? He evidently sees the immensity of the material universe vanishing as a frightening spiritual pressure makes itself felt.[36] He speaks of the force that holds the universe together as so gripping the world "that the monads will pour into that place whither they are irrevocably destined by the total maturing of all things and the implacable irreversibility of the whole history of the world—some of them spiritualized matter in the limitless fulfillment of an eternal communion, and others materialized spirit in the conscious agonies of an interminable decomposition."[37] Thus the End is no natural growth of the world into the Kingdom of God but a catastrophic convulsion in which human maturation and Point Omega meet, so that "a descendant divine involution would come to combine with the ascendant cosmic evolution."[38] We have a natural process moving to its consummation by the active operation within it of the Christ who is both its energizing and its attractive center. In the Incarnation we have a renewal and restoration of all the forces of the Universe, and Christ is "the instrument, the center, the end of all animate and material Creation."[39]

The more one examines statements like these, the more there is a sense of ambiguity. On the one hand, Teilhard seems to believe that all the elements of the world will be transfigured. To support this viewpoint, we have a sentence in a letter to Pere Auguste Valensin: Christ "must at the same time sustain and bring to their ultimate perfection the material strata of the world . . ."[40] On the other hand, the general burden of his thought would appear to be that the tangential component of energy shall move to ultimate dissolution, and the radial component, already increasingly taking over throughout the process, shall move to its ultimate perfecting and fulfillment in the hyperpersonal. This stage calls for the world and its elements attaining a critical point of annihilation. So Teilhard speaks of the End as "the death of the materially exhausted universe; the split of the noosphere, divided on the form to be given to its unity; and simultaneously . . . the liberation of that percentage of the universe which, across time, space and evil, will have succeeded in laboriously synthesizing itself to the very end."[41] Again, does he in the last phrase suggest that even the world apart from man, man's natural environment, may in some sense have a contribution to bring to the ultimate Kingdom?

From the point of view of ultimate eschatology, Teilhard makes like contribution to our ecological crisis. The population burst is rather thought of as creating the pressures that lead to the final human maturation. The Second Law of Thermodynamics means ultimate decomposition of the physical, and our own present wastefulness is hastening the day when the Parousia will mean a catastrophic advent of the hyperpersonal and the Beyond. Yet we have a feeling that this does not do justice to Teilhard's concern for nature and man's physical and biological environment. We find him vigorously attacking the way in which man wastes the earth's resources. He reminds us that food supply and population burst raise serious issues and asks how long science will take to provide food by direct synthesis of the chemical elements. "The population graph is rising almost vertically, while useable land in every continent is being ruined for lack of proper husbandry. We must take care: we still have feet of clay!"[42] Yet he hopefully speaks of the human race redressing and rectifying themselves as the pressure increases, rather than being stultified by overcrowding. Again, the ambiguity! Does all this portend the nearness of Omega Point, or will our efforts to deal faithfully with our environment be one dimension of what the ultimate consummation will achieve?

THE THEOLOGY OF HOPE AND THE RECOVERY OF ESCHATOLOGY

In Germany the philosophy of Ernst Bloch has stimulated much thought and provided a basis for the rediscovery of Christian eschatology. Aware of the need for dynamic categories in theological thought, that the emphasis on evolution and history calls for a view of the universe as a developing process, that the current this-worldly concern and the scientific empiricist preoccupation place their emphasis on this world and not on any supernatural or transcendent order, and that the issue of transcendence has become critical because of the failure of spatial models to communicate, many theologians have turned to the new Marxist humanism for inspiration. They include Jürgen Moltmann, Wolfhart Pannenberg, Johannes Metz, Edward Schillebeeckx, and Karl Rahner—all German.[43] In this country Carl Braaten[44] and others are becoming increasingly interested in this theological approach.

The two leading exponents have been Moltmann and Pannenberg. Each in his own way, but with increasing unanimity, has sought to adopt the insights of the philosophy of hope to the theological concerns of Christian theism. Moltmann has been more directly influenced by Bloch. Pannenberg also shows the impact of the newly awakened interest in Hegel. Both place the emphasis on the historical process and on the future as a viable model for divine transcendence. Both have reinstated Christian eschatology in a dominant place in Christian thought. Both put more emphasis on the Cross and the Resurrection than on the Incarnation, and this despite the fact that Pannenberg has produced a very competent and stimulating book on the latter, one of the most significant German contributions since the work of the Protestant giants of the last century. This might be expected in the Lutheran tradition, whereas there are strong influences of Anglican and Catholic theology in the views that we have just discussed.

A part of our difficulty with this group of thinkers is that their theological approach has much to offer to our own particular problem, for it is secular, takes history seriously in the historian's sense of the word, and sees a future for this world structure within its eschatological emphasis. Yet its exponents have little to say about the scientific picture of the world, about evolution, or about man's relationship to nature. Some members of the circle are, however, manifesting an interest in the work of the late Karl Heim, understandably since he emphasized the "already-become" and the "not-yet-become." What we propose to do is to map out relevant areas of their thought and draw some implications. Again, because of the many exponents, we shall endeavor to emphasize their agreements and pass over the more insignificant differences.

Concerned to speak to a world which has become increasingly secularized, aware that a two-tier universe with a supernatural and invisible order supervening upon the natural and visible has no relevance to scientifically oriented man, such thinkers seek to give the divine transcendence a temporal rather than a spatial model. They do so by placing their emphasis upon an aspect of Christian theologizing which has been often either misinterpreted or neglected —the eschatological future. No one can say that the eschatological has not been emphasized in certain quarters, but the emphasis has often been accompanied by a neglect of its future aspect and a concern with its realization in the person of Jesus of Nazareth. We have seen this in the very differing approaches of C. H. Dodd and Rudolf Bultmann. What has happened now is a rediscovery of the biblical emphasis on the future and on apocalypticism, made more viable by a philosophical reliance on the thought of Hegel and of Ernst Bloch. The divine transcendence is presented to us in terms of a temporal future. God transcends his world as its absolute future, he to whom the whole process is moving.

In this kind of thinking time and history become central. Words like "hope," "promise," "future" become pregnant with theological meaning. The prime reality is not nature but history. The revelation of God is in history. Pannenberg is very emphatic that the revelation is history, a very Hegelian standpoint. Moltmann makes much more of the special stream of revelation history. Both attack Bultmann and Barth and contend that there must be no differentiation between *Historie* and *Geschichte*. The revelation is in historical actuality as historians understand it, and there is no dualism in their thinking. For Pannenberg, faith must not impose meaning on history but must find meaning in history. Moltmann would acquiesce but is much more aware that meaning comes both in and *through* history.

Both Pannenberg and Moltmann are concerned with the historical roots of faith, and are especially concerned with the historical actuality of the Resurrection. Pannenberg, in particular, spends much time demonstrating the authenticity of the Resurrection.[45] For these thinkers this event is the kingpin of their structure, the point at which the *eschaton* towards which all history is moving has become especially operative within the process. For Pannenberg, all history is the field of the divine activity. His emphasis falls on universal history, and he sees God as the transcendent presence hidden within it, the powerful "future" who can only be understood and fully revealed in the ultimate consummation. ". . . the unity of the world is to be expected from its future."[46] This powerful future has been manifested in Jesus of Nazareth, but even the meaning that faith finds in him arises from the historical actuality of the Resurrection. Christology must begin from below and not from above, from the future actualized in the Resurrection and not from some transcendent aboveness.[47]

One interesting aspect of the thought especially of Pannenberg is his dialogue with process theology. As well as to Hegel, his thought is indebted to Alfred North Whitehead. He emphasizes the contingent aspect of the events of the world-process and notes the ambiguity of the future, its unpredictability and lively indefiniteness. But he holds that as the process moves forward, "the ambiguity of the impending future congeals into finite and definite fact."[48] The infinite future is thus continually separating itself from the already-become, letting go of itself to bring about our ever-moving present. This thought echoes the ideas of Karl Heim[49] who, as does Pannenberg, used it to explain away deterministic and mechanistic causation. The present is determined by the power of the future, which is neither a void nor a bundle of chances. The absolute future is a powerful personal God who holds together in unity the whole process. Pannenberg declares that: "The notion of the Kingdom of God evokes a vision of the unity of each being and the unity of the whole world as flowing from the future."[50] There is an abundant and powerful future which transcends all finite happenings and determines the specific essence of everything. The process must not be understood in terms of creation alone but in the light of eschatology also.

Hence Pannenberg can accept the Whiteheadian view of "the ultimate elements of reality in terms of single occasions contingently following each other."[51] But while he accepts the thesis of the prehension of other occasions within the satisfaction of a particular actual occasion, he holds that the position would be better expressed if the contingency of new events or occasions were ascribed to the futuristic power of creative love. Presumably he implies that the mental pole of an actual entity should be directed on the future, to which the creativity in matter and also the eternal objects should be ascribed. The absolute future determines the creative movement and actual being of all things. God the fellow traveler is replaced by God the power of the future.

At this point also the theology of hope enters another caveat. God is not dipolar as Whitehead and Hartshorne contend.[52] There is no development in God. From the standpoint of the finite present, the future is undecided, and truth is decided within the movement of time, even the truth with regard to the divine essence. Truth that becomes evident in the future will have been true all the time. So, with God, he is present now as he will be manifest in the future, even though the truth about him waits for its full unveiling.

It is clear that for Pannenberg and Moltmann, too, all the emphasis falls on the future. Even creation cannot be divorced from eschatology. It is ends, not origins, that count. God has separated a part of reality from himself. Because he is love, he has granted it existence and contingency. Because he is creative love, he is continually eventuating the new and releasing the contingent from his absolute future. Because he is love, he is synthesizing and reconciling his creation, drawing it into unity as the power of the future. The creative power is the unifying power. "The events in their relation to one another participate in the love that created them. Each preliminary integration among events and that from which they eventuated emerges as an anticipation of an ultimate unity."[53] There is a strong Hegelian flavor in this, without Hegel's association of becoming with the divine self-determination!

The process of evolution becomes, in this thinking, a manifestation of the power of the future. Creatures move forward to ever new participation in the creative and powerful future that ever lies ahead. Organisms are relating themselves to the future which can and will change their present condition, yet, below man, they are not *"aware* of the future of (their) own future."[54] Such a quality is reserved for man.

The thought is Christocentric since in the Resurrection the power of the future is manifested. As the unique manifestation of the absolute future, the Christ is he in whom all things were created and in whom all things will be gathered up. ". . . as the eschatological summation of the world process to a unity, Jesus is the mediator of creation. As such, . . . he is . . . the reconciler of the cosmos."[55] The eschatological revelation of God in Jesus Christ means that he gathers the whole process into a unity of history. Pannenberg can thus declare that "the incarnation of God in Jesus of Nazareth forms the point of reference in relation to which the world's course has its unity and on the basis of which every event and every figure in creation is what it is."[56] The creation of the world is indeed fulfilled through his resurrection, and through that event Jesus exercises his Lordship over the whole world-process.

Where it comes to practical outreach Moltmann has much to say. We have emphasized Pannenberg so far because his treatment is free from the dialogue with Bloch which often preoccupies Moltmann. The latter does reflect Bloch's approach more explicitly, although the parallel in Pannenberg's thinking is very evident. Moltmann likewise sees God as the power of the future, the God who promises that he will make all things new. This promise is reflected in the Exodus out of Egypt, but the Exodus of Jesus Christ from the dead secures that promise in the historical process. The Cross shows what history is, but the Resurrection gives us the promise of that God who is the power of the future. These two opposing realities in the history of Jesus of Nazareth disclose the basic contradiction between present history and the future promise of God. Once more we see Jesus as reconciler and the promise of the ultimate unity of the process.

Moltmann then sees the Church as the Exodus church, created within history by the Resurrection. Its specific mission is to bear testimony to the future of God and to prepare the way for the coming Kingdom. Men are called to a discipleship which means "to join in working for the Kingdom of God that is to come."[57] The Christian sees in history the contradiction inherent in this unredeemed world, and the Cross is a reminder that his Christian mission and his Christian hope must be a way of suffering. Always he is beckoned on to Christ's future and the future of Christ's Lordship. Hence he must offer at cost a reconciliation for man, and, presumably, for the world too. This "obedience" to truth involves the dimensions of social transformation, and, by implication, man's relation to his natural environment. Man is to institute community, set things right and put them in order, work for righteousness and peace, because he sees that these are involved in Christ's future, the future that is the power of God. So Moltmann can speak of " 'creative expectation,' hope which sets about criticizing and transforming the present because it is open to the universal future of the Kingdom."[58] The world is not yet finished. It is engaged in a history standing under the horizon of a new future, already manifested in Christ.

This theology has the merit of being concerned with this world-structure and thus of speaking to the secular attitudes of our time. In majoring upon a temporal and futuristic model for the divine transcendence, it avoids the spatial and two-tier approach so repugnant to many of our contemporaries. Furthermore, it brings in the eschatological dimension. Yet it lacks theological balance, for often it so stresses God as the power of the future that it tends to minimize the past and present divine activity. The creative and recreative movement of the immanent Spirit is almost by-passed, especially by Moltmann. The Incarnation is given such a proleptic coloring that some of the rich insights which it offers to thinkers like Pittenger and Teilhard are lost. The understanding of creation undoubtedly gains when it is harnessed to the eschatological dimension, but we hear little of God rejoicing at the work of his hands in and for itself, with all its potentialities. That the world is ever moving to unity in the future is only one aspect, for, despite evil and dysteleology, it does possess harmonious and aesthetic qualities even now.

One has the feeling that this approach has seized upon the fact that modern man is much more oriented to the future than to the past, that, in some sense, he is posthistoric. Yet does one have to sell out a full orbed theological program in order to accommodate oneself to the modern temper? The theological truth will always have a cause of stumbling, and, in such accommodations, dimensions of God may be lost which modern man needs. It is one thing to contend that we must speak to our time. It is another so to concentrate on a favorite aspect that other theological insights are lost. God is the God of the past and the present, as well as the future. Other models for transcendence are possible, such as in process thought, and these pay much more attention to other dimensions of the Incarnation and the present moment of the world-process. We can be grateful for the eschatological emphasis and we need to keep it, but this theology has exaggerated one aspect of the divine reality to the impoverishment of the full understanding of God. Furthermore, to major on the Resurrection tends to put in the shadow the full impact of the life and death of Jesus of Nazareth, without which the meaning of the Resurrection is lost. Christ as the incorporating man was all his life activated by an incarnate love of which the Cross and Resurrection were the consummation. Pannenberg makes more of this than does Moltmann.

One significant aspect of this eschatological emphasis is its activism. It does not call for a quiescent waiting for the Kingdom. God brings the Kingdom, but the Christian is also a co-worker in that coming. We are called to work in creative expectation and thereby change the pattern of this world and its structures. Man is set free by the Gospel of the coming Kingdom to labor and to suffer. As Metz reminds us: "Christian eschatology is . . . a productive and militant eschatology, which gradually realizes itself. Since Christian hope (is that very hope which) does not only eat its stew but must also brew its stew. An eschatological faith and an engagement in the world do not exclude one another."[59] Again he writes: "The power of God's promises for the future moves us to form this world into the eschatological city of God."[60] Although the major concern of such thinkers is with man's social structures, what they say at this point is very relevant to our ecological ventures.

FIVE

Theology and Ecology

WE MUST NOW SEEK TO DEVELOP A THEOLOGY of nature in dialogue with the positions already outlined. Their concern with this world not only reflects the secular attitude of our day and the contemporary scientific approach to our world, but it is also in keeping with the world-affirming nature of the Christian faith itself and of the Judaic tradition within which it came to birth. The facts that the Christian understanding of God is bound up with a divine self-disclosure in history, that at the center of such an understanding there is the Incarnation with its affirmation that God lifted one human life into the very center of his own personal being and made the actuality of historical existence ingredient in his own life, that the Christian faith sees this world as the theater within which God's purpose is fulfilled within the historical life of the creatures, and that in the creation story of Genesis 1 God is presented as celebrating his world and declaring it to be good—all these point to the significance of both nature and history in the divine purpose.

The biblical approach to man sees him as a psychosomatic whole, in which the bodily form and structure is ingredient to the totality of the divine image in man. Man's response to God, with which the model of the divine image is concerned, involves cooperation with God in this world. The Genesis story sees one dimension of such a model in man's control over nature and in human fertility. Man is created to multiply and also to subdue the earth. That he has carried out the first, capacity ad nauseum is a reminder that man has not used his sexual powers under the divine aegis. That he is a scientist carries with it the reminder that scientific knowledge is a divine gift. That he has mismanaged his gift and caused environmental chaos points to the fact that such a gift can be rightly exercised only with some degree of acknowledgment of its source, however vague and possibly only at the level of moral responsibility. Yet again, for Jesus the forgiveness of sins had relation to the whole man, and new life with God meant a new system of relationships to the world. In our Lord's healing miracles this is very evident—to put a man in right relationship with God could mean the righting of his bodily and mental condition.

If all this is a true understanding of the Christian stance, then science and secularity need all the support that the Christian can give. The Church in its prophetic ministry stands here as the conscience of the community—or, it ought to do so—pointing to the overarching purpose of the God whom it serves and who has given to man his capacities for scientific achievement. The Christian cannot contract out of his responsibilities to his fellow-men. He is intimately related to both his natural environment and his social setting. They constitute the world into which God has "thrown" him. They provide the nexus of relationships within which he is to live out the life with Christ and in God. Because of this, he must have a theological approach to nature and an ethical concern for nature grounded in his understanding of God.

Any such theological approach must begin with the disclosure of God. So often our theological approach has begun with man and his sin rather than with God and his redeeming love. The Incarnation has too often been accounted for on the basis of man's sinful condition rather than as the culmination of God's creative act. Despairing of man, impregnated with ideas of man's total depravity, recognizing nothing good in the human race, theologians have turned to Christ as a way out, an escape mechanism, a gap filler for the deficiencies of the human race. God, we are told, has "broken in," but has not God as Creator Spirit been immanent throughout? Furthermore, is there nothing we can say about the moral ideals, religious visions, elevating thoughts of our "depraved" humanity? Must we reject humanism at its best, or may not God be working in diverse ways in the human conscience, the religious consciousness, the noble philosophical systems, the intellectual achievements of the human race? So often we have sacrificed a true Christian theism on the altar of deism and spoken of a kind of absentee God who has consigned his world to darkness, has entered it in Christ, and is snatching his church out of it. Our eschatology has become correspondingly individualistic with no cosmic and social dimensions. The world becomes a stage across which individual souls make their pilgrimage to the heavenly city, but in which nature and history serve no other ultimate purpose.

This is no honest interpretation of the biblical witness. We need to ask ourselves whether the Incarnation was necessitated by sin or whether it is primarily the event in which the full purpose of the whole creative process is unveiled. Here is redemptive love—yes— but redemptive love as an expression of that love which rejoices in its whole creation including man himself. No thinking man can ignore the reality of sin and the demonic. But to magnify God at the expense of man does a strange disservice to the divine purpose of love and the implications of the Incarnation. Jesus did not address men as if they were incapable of response. He spoke of them as God's children and made ethical demands with the evident assumption that they did possess a potential for responsive conduct. Faith, for Paul, might be God's gift but it was also man's decision. There is sad need theologically for a Christian humanism which celebrates God's love but does not minimize man's God-given capacities.

Over a century ago F. D. Maurice[1] could declare that theology must not begin with man and his sin, measuring the straight line by the crooked one. It must begin with Christ in whom God has created and redeemed mankind. "Mankind stands not in Adam but in Christ,"[2] he could write. He reiterated this key thought again and again, although he never gave a consistent logical development of it so as to produce a theological system. God has united himself with the human race in Christ, and it is from Christ that all other facts must be interpreted. We may not agree with the way in which Maurice developed his theological understanding, but we need his theological chiding. Even in dealing with nature, we must begin with Christ and understand creation in the light of Incarnation. The world was not created in Adam and does not stand in his obedience but rather "it stood and stands in the obedience of God's well-beloved Son; the real image of the Father, the real bond of human society and of the whole universe, who was to be manifested in the fullness of time, as that which He had always been."[3]

THE INCARNATION AS DIVINE DISCLOSURE

If we follow Maurice's advice, we start with the divine self-giving in Jesus of Nazareth. We move from God to his world. Now it is true that the ultimate awakening of faith came with the Resurrection. Pannenberg's argument that this historical event awoke men to the truth of the Incarnation and that therefore the latter must be understood from below and not from above is a valid one. Did not Paul confess that the Christ was declared to be the Son of God with power by the resurrection from the dead? Yet this is not the full answer, for the impact of the life played its part in the disclosure of God through Jesus' humanity alongside the impact of the Cross and the Resurrection. The point to note is that men came to recognize a dimension of depth in this man which separated him from his fellows. Here was a unique and transforming divine disclosure. This man stood as verily Son of God. Jesus was Immanuel—God with us.

Bonhoeffer wrote of Christ: "The key to everything is 'in him.' All that we may rightly expect from God and pray for is to be found in Jesus Christ."[4] Now it is true that we can emphasize our Christocentric concern so much that we find ourselves left with a Christomonism. The Wisdom Literature of the Old Testament and the religious experience of mankind should warn us against this kind of exclusiveness. That God has and does reveal himself elsewhere is not in dispute, but from the point of view of the Christian under-

standing of God and his world we have to find our focal point in
the Christ and in the Christ in his personal unity as God-man. However we may seek to explain and build models for the Christological
mystery, the truth remains much as it was boldly stated at Chalce-
don that this being, Jesus of Nazareth, is both truly man and truly
God. As such, he is for faith the final disclosure of God and the unveiling of the true being of man.

Let us note that as such the Christ is contemporaneous with and
accompanies all our times. In him God has gathered one human
life uniquely into his life, but because he is, in the unity of his person, both God and man, his life is not past to us. The truth of the
Resurrection is that his humanity has become in all its actuality a
part of the life of God. It has been pointed out that when we speak
of Jesus Christ, we should speak with the same breath of his deity
and of his *risen* humanity. Thereby we can speak of the Christ as
Lord of all history and of all nature. He did not shed his humanity
at death, but it was raised in the unity of his God-manhood. Thereby
he comes to us still as God-man. Bonhoeffer, among his many theological insights, saw this and stated it clearly: "The presence of
Christ necessitates the statement 'Jesus is fully man'—and it necessitates the other statement, 'Jesus is fully God.' "[5] We must not
isolate the man Jesus from the unity of the God-man. "God in time-
less eternity is not God, Jesus limited by time is not Jesus. Rather
God is God in the man Jesus. In this Jesus Christ God is present."[6]
If we strip the ascension of its spatial imagery, this is what it signifies theologically. When we speak of the Holy Spirit, this is what
we mean theologically—the continuing immanent presence of the
God-man, Jesus Christ, in his risen humanity.

This historical actuality discloses to us the nature of God as personal love. Whatever God may be beyond and above this, he is personal, and in his essential being, he shows himself to be love. He
shows himself as this, both in the original historical disclosure and
in the continuing presence of the Christ in the Church. Men have
come to know in Christ a love which forgives and reconciles, a love
which sets them free to be their true selves. In all speculative attempts to reach deeper into the mystery behind this disclosure, men
have never escaped the reality of that love which reaches out to

them from its midst. The triune God, out of his depth as Father
and in his eternal personal modes as Son and Spirit, is ever a trinity
of love, a personal unity of love.

But Jesus reminds us that such a God *accompanies* his creation.
However we are to think of transcendence these days, it has become increasingly evident that the old spatial models have little
relevance in our day. We have already discussed this. It is the
merit of the process theologians that they have reminded us of another model, for it is fitting that if God comes to us as personal, we
seek for a model of his presence and absence, his immanence and
transcendence at this level. When we begin with the personal self-
transcendence of finite beings like ourselves, we may legitimately
think of God as the personal self-transcendent depth of this infinite
universe. Of course the model is an analogy. It must not be taken
literally and thus applied at every point. The world is not God's body.
It is quasi-independent, with natural contingencies and human freedom. But we may think of the divine transcendence as a personal
depth of love which is yet also immanent and present in every part
of the universe, just as we both transcend ourselves and yet are
present in every aspect of our psychosomatic whole. This model has
real significance when we come shortly to consider the relation of
God to the natural process. It does remove all thoughts of a two-
tier universe and speak to the secularity so dominant in our day.

If the electron needs two models for its understanding—the wave
and the particle—we might expect that one model will not suffice
to understand the infinite personhood of God. Now at the personal
level, we need to remember another kind of transcendence—the
intrapersonal. Increasingly theologians are recognizing the transcendence of personhood and thus the otherness, hiddenness, transcendence that is present in all personal, I-Thou, relationships. As
Buber[7] has continually stressed, the I-Thou relationship is one in
which both parties have to descend from the egoistic throne and
enter into existential encounter. The Thou sets limits to the I, for
it has its own claims and its own will. While the Thou is open to
and for the I, it also is free from the I. Personality, its freedom and
its capacity for decision, means that history escapes from any general laws that a historian may try to impose. The person is free, in-

accessible to my thinking and my prediction. Here is a hidden reality. Thus we have a mutual transcendence, and yet also a mutual indwelling which disclosure and responding love and empathy make possible. Once more we have a model for transcendence.[8] If all personal being involves such transcendence, how much more the absolute Person, who both transcends us in his hiddenness yet indwells us and all his creatures in his givenness. God above all his finite creatures has the capacity of at the same time being-for and being-free-from the other.

Yet a third model presents itself. The transcendence of the personal lies in a limited way in a certain control over one's future. But the "absolute Personal" has his own future and the future of all his creatures in his hands. He is the absolute future, and here we can be indebted to the theologians of hope.

Now if we major on one model we may build a consistent system, but we may also miss some deep and rich insights which the Incarnation offers to us in its divine disclosure. We have tried to suggest this in our critique of the theology of hope. Yet all these models have something to say about nature as well as man, and all offer, when they are pursued, insights which give a deeper understanding of the divine involvement in the process of nature as well as in that of history. If the electron needs two models, need we be surprised that our understanding of the Creator of the electron, in all his personal hiddenness and transcendence, may not require more! What all, in some sense, say to us is present there in the Incarnation. Bonhoeffer saw this. Christ is for us and yet he transcends us in his freedom. In his contemporaneous presence he is still the man-for-others, but he is God-man, and in the freedom of his self-giving he absolutely transcends us. As Bonhoeffer again reminds us: "God is *beyond* in the midst of our life."[9] To be concerned for other persons is to experience transcendence, and thus we must not seek God apart from the world but in the world. We must meet the Christ in the world around us, in other persons, and in nature too. He is Christ for us, touching us in his risen humanity and embracing the whole world in it. We need to look at the sacramental implications of this later in this chapter. Hence God comes to us in the midst of the world, in what we know. Authentic transcendence, Bonhoeffer could claim, implies a relation to God that "is a new life in 'existence for others,' through participation in the being of Jesus."[10] In varying ways these models point to such an understanding.

The disclosure of the Incarnation reminds us too of the way that God comes to us. He comes to us through the mediation of his created order and remains hidden behind the world which he has called into being. His presence is always a mediated presence, in and through the creatures—nature, men, and history. This is the mode of his coming in the biblical testimony, but it is also evident in all religions. That he comes down in the deep places of man's self-consciousness is also true, but what has sometimes been called the mystical a priori is the premise of that deeper and more defined apprehension to which the divine disclosure in and through our world awakens us. The awareness of God meeting us within is that point of contact by which the God who meets us without exercises his leverage on our personal being. But his disclosing presence without through the realm of nature, through prophetic personalities and saintly lives, through the movements of history and societies of believers gives clearer definition to our understanding of him. This revelatory presence is brought to a focus in Jesus of Nazareth, where the living God has brought our human life intimately into union with his own and made one human life transparent to his presence. Tillich has made the point that, wherever the medium of the divine presence becomes so totally surrendered to that which it discloses that it annihilates itself, we have a final revelation. This can be said of Jesus, but we must not separate the obedience to death from the resurrection. Here men's eyes are opened and they see into the depth of the universe as this is opened up for them in the God-man. Such a disclosure is final in the sense that, within our finite and creaturely order, this is the supreme manifestation of the "transcendent presence," even though it may not be final in time. The eschaton, the end of all history, has become incarnate. In the death and resurrection of Jesus of Nazareth, the pattern of the divine life has become evident.

Let it be noted that this does not eliminate the divine presence in and disclosure through nature. Rather it illuminates it. The degree of revelation in nature—the divine qualities that are dis-

closed—is not at the same level as is possible through human personality, least of all when that personality is so committed to God
that it possesses oneness with the transcendent presence. We see
God coming to us everywhere when our eyes have been opened to
his presence in the living Christ in his risen humanity.

Furthermore, the truth in the theology of hope becomes evident,
if we recognize that, even though the *eschaton* be incarnate in Jesus
of Nazareth, yet the God who in the future will be fully unveiled is
here hidden and incognito. We sing "veiled in the flesh the Godhead
see," but see as through a glass darkly. We walk by faith and not
by sight. In this sense God is our absolute future, and the "incarnate
eschaton" is given to us in promise. Yet this is no reason why we
should regard transcendence in purely temporal and futuristic
terms. Once we acknowledge that in a *real* sense the transcendent
future is also present, it would seem to this writer that the other
two models which we have indicated would have to be called in to
make such presence intelligible. The "absolute future" accompanies
all time and is incarnate in Jesus, his life, death, and resurrection.

This indicates the truths which the process thinkers are stressing.
If God be the living God, if he be personal, if the world-process
is bound up with his will and purpose, then surely that process is
significant in what we may call his experience. Above all, does not
the Incarnation, by positing that one human life is in its totality
also the life of God, say much about the nature of God himself?
When we talk about the risen humanity of the Christ, about the
presence of Christ as the God-man who accompanies the life of our
world, we are implying that what happens in our world is also integral to the life of God himself. To speak of the Cross as the manifestation of suffering and redeeming love points to that Cross as
ingredient in the divine experience, however much dominant Greek
influences and the Sabellian heresy may have led the early church
to condemn "Patripassianism." The prophets of the Old Testament
testify to God's feeling and compassion and were not averse to a
noble higher anthropomorphism. The Apostle Paul thinks of the
divine spirit interceding for us *with sighs* (Rom. 8:26). The Incarnation in its totality, Cross and Resurrection as its climax, brings
to a focus in the actuality of history that redemptive suffering love

with which God accompanies and guides the whole creative process and gathers it into his own life. The God who is eternally love is himself enriched as his purpose is actualized in a process to which he has given its varying degrees of being and its quasi independence. As he suffers with it and rejoices in it, he redemptively guides it to its ultimate consummation, gathered around his own incarnate presence with its risen humanity. Thus ever perfect, his is a growing perfection of love, enriched as that love becomes actualized in a creative and redemptive world-process. In that redemptive act he calls his children to be his fellow workers. This brings us at once to the place and function of nature.

The Creative Process and the Natural Order

The biblical witness points to God as Creator. As we have seen, there are two strands—one based on human observation and the other upon the divine disclosure of God as redemptive love. The latter is the more significant, and, in the New Testament, it projects the Christ backward to the beginnings of the creative process. The Incarnation becomes the key to the creative as well as the redemptive aspects of the whole created order. He who redemptively creates the new man is behind the creation of the first man. He who remakes the world was involved in the making of that world. The Christ is he in whom all things were created.

This idea of the preexistent Christ is theologically significant quite apart from its Trinitarian implications and their accompanying speculations. The latter are often claimed to be a stumbling block to the modern mind, and undoubtedly the New Testament witnesses were casting their understanding into the thought forms which their own contemporary Hellenistic situation provided. Yet there are certain theological truths which such an idea expresses.[11]

For one thing it reminds us that the self-emptying of the Incarnation was, in a very real sense, continuous with the whole creative process and within the divine creative intention. Jesus the Christ is the bringing to a focus of the truth which underlies the whole creation in all its long history. It is not just the Incarnation that is the gracious self-giving of the divine love nor does God just pour himself into his creation in the redemptive self-giving of Jesus. The whole creative process is a manifestation of the self-emptying and self-limitation of the divine being. God wills that he shall share the mystery of his being by granting existence and being to a world. He grants it being and quasi independence. He gives it a share of his own freedom and creativity. Out of his depth of being as Father he comes forth as creative and redemptive Word, pouring being into a created order in which contingency and freedom are ingredient. He wills to allow finite beings to participate in his infinite being, and his love finds expression in a created order into which it may be poured. This Word, this coming forth of God in creative activity, finds its supreme expression in the Incarnate Christ. It takes flesh within the created order and through one man pours itself redemptively into the process. Thus, in this historic actuality, we see unveiled the creative self-giving that originated the whole process. We see the Creator as one who, through his Word, in all the travail of creating is giving himself, emptying himself in love. Jesus is the "infleshment" of this Word, the divine being as he is continuously coming forth in creative and redemptive expression. When we look at Jesus and his resurrection, we know that all creation exists as such an expression. The Christ is the unveiling of the creative intention. As creative Word he is before all things. All that we see in him is in the divine intention. The whole process that led to his historical actuality is the expression of that creative Word which is embodied in him.

This implies that the Christ was not just necessitated by man's sin but is the climax of the whole process. Thus a second implication of the preexistence theme is that, at the level of his humanity, the Christ completes the divine creation. He is man as God intended him to be, man living in complete union with the divine. But this humanity is the objective of the whole creative movement. The Christ preexists in the sense that the whole process is directed towards bringing him forth; it prefigures him. Potential within the movement there are all the possibilities that are actualized in his humanity. In his Godward aspect, the Christ expresses the truth behind the whole process of God's self-giving, self-emptying love and embodies the divine Word that comes forth as creative expression of the divine being. Now, we are suggesting that, in his man-ward aspect, the Christ is the goal of the whole process, prefigured throughout its long development—his perfect humanity was the inner meaning of all creation. The potentialities which attained actualization in him were present in the process from the beginning. We are here echoing the thought of Teilhard, who sees the whole process directed towards Omega Point and finds such a Point Omega already achieved within the process in the Incarnation. To quote John Macquarrie: ". . . Christ brings to actualization the potentialities for being that belong to the creation. He does so by bringing creaturely being to the point where it is at one with the expressive Being of God, the point where the Word is made flesh."[12]

If we think of Christ in his humanity as the climax of the evolutionary process and not as simply a divine strategy for dealing with human sin, as within God's creative intention quite apart from the actuality of evil and human estrangement, we have a much richer understanding of the function of the Incarnation in this world. Furthermore, we do not have to confine his significance to man but may expand it to the whole natural order. Both creatively and redemptively, he is at the center of the whole cosmos.

This becomes clear if we see man as in some sense a microcosm of the macrocosm. This theme is central in Teilhard's understanding of the process of evolution. He sees it moving from the physical level through the biosphere to the noosphere. But every new level builds upon and embodies what is contained at the lower levels. The noosphere is possible only because it embraces the achievements of the process at the lower levels of the biosphere and the cosmosphere. As the basic energy attains more complex formulation, as its interior or inner aspect becomes more significant, as cerebralization moves to its climax, we see the creative emergence of man himself. And man embodies in himself the structures of the physiochemical level including the complex chromosomes or DNA molecules, the cellular structures without which life would be impossible, the psychological and neural structures which are increasingly centralized in the cerebrum. Man is, as has well been said, an amphibian. He is a part of nature, and yet he transcends nature. He is matter, but he is also spirit. He is a psychosomatic whole, but he is also self-transcendent. He has a capacity which no other creature seems to have. He knows, but he also knows that he knows. He is in the process of nature and yet transcends it, and to some degree, can control it.

Now if man sums up the whole natural process in his own imperfect being, how much more may we say this of the him who manifested in his own humanity the true destiny of the human race! This would suggest that nature has a significant role in the divine purpose and that we have no right so to concentrate upon man's spiritual dimension that we neglect his oneness with the natural process out of which he ·has creatively emerged. Furthermore, we cannot limit the regenerative and re-creative activity of the Incarnate Word solely to man. Paul saw the whole creation travailing in pain together, waiting for unveiling of those sons of God who achieve their sonship in the Christ (Rom. 8:22, 23). In Paul Tillich's memorable quotation from Schelling, "Nature, also, mourns for a lost good."[13] The Christian hope is not concerned with the immortality of disembodied spirits but with the resurrection of the body. The biblical witnesses point to a consummation in which a new, re-created, resurrected heaven and earth shall participate. The Christ is cosmic in his sweep! In his own true and risen humanity, he unveils the true meaning of all creation and gives promise of its glorious future. Nature has its own meaning for God. He rejoiced in it on the morn of creation, not just because it should be a habitat for men made in his image, but also because it had its own life and reflected back to him some facets of that outpoured love which he lavished upon his creation. This is no fanciful pleading, for the Incarnation points to it.

What then are we to say about this physical order? It has often been pointed out that the emergence of self-conscious spirit in the process, with its apprehension of absolute values, says a great deal about the process itself. Two alternatives face us—either a reductionism which explains the spiritual in terms of the physical or a recognition that what appears as the physical has some degree of kinship with the spiritual which emerges within it and can control it. Each in their own way, both the process theologians and evolutionary theologians like Teilhard have recognized this. We find Whitehead and his followers adopting a panpsychic stance and,

Whitehead in particular, rejecting the fallacy of misplaced concreteness! Nature must not be reduced to a system of chunks of matter, located in space, moving in time, and linked together by a network of mechanical causation. Rather the whole process must be understood in terms of an organic model. It must be pictured as an organism embracing lesser organisms at various levels of being, bound together by a network of prehensions, sensitive to one another and fulfilling their own particular role within that prehensive setting. We are asked to see the creative process as alive, dynamic, creative, manifesting at even its lowest level of reality a capacity for feeling, however rudimentary. What appears to be the physical is actually capable of a very low level of psychic response.

Teilhard likewise points to an inner dimension or component of energy which works within and alongside of the physical. He is careful to remind us that science only offers a true explanation of nature when it includes man himself with all his mental and spiritual capacities. In his own way he is suggesting, like Whitehead, that science treats nature as a closed box dominated by mechanistic causation and that this is an abstraction. Such an abstraction is possible only when the consequences of human activity and the part which human intervention plays in the process are ignored or eliminated. As T. E. Jessop reminds us: Nature "is a closed system only as presented by the sciences, which on principle, for the sake of intellectual tidiness, ignore man's action in it and on it, and thereby turn it into an abstraction, a neat fiction, a logical whole but an unreality."[14] But, on the ecological level, it is precisely the fact that man can intervene in the process of nature, reshape it, even create something artificial and perhaps destructive, which provides the crux of our problem. Teilhard puts his finger upon the basic issue in his dictum that, with the emergence of man, the process has become self-conscious and thus able to take over the direction of its evolutionary drive.

On the basis of this emergence of man's mental and spiritual capacities, Teilhard makes it a model by which to understand "energy." The radial component of the latter, quiescent at the beginning of the process, produces increasing interiorization with the emergence of life, mind, and self-conscious spirit. At the same time, the physical component, responsible for the increasing complexity of the developing structure, becomes also increasingly subservient to it. That Teilhard would seem to have nature and the physical drop away like a chrysalis in the final consummation is incidental at this point. But he is suggesting that whatever energy be, it has that in it which is responsive to mind and which carries the potentiality for emergent spirit.

The thinkers just referred to have much to say about our ecological problem. Science sees nature bound together in a not always perfect ecological balance, which man with his science and technology has increasingly disturbed. The biblical testimony points to a covenant structure in which man is bound to his natural environment as well as to God and his fellow-men. Failure to observe this covenant bond leads to disaster for both him and his natural habitat. Now we find two groups of philosophical theologians emphasizing the same truth, picturing nature at all levels, even the physical, as possessing psychic characteristics, capable of sensitivity and responsiveness, and as having potentialities hidden in the seeming physical which can become actualized as life and mind.

Martin Buber[15] has emphasized the distinction between the I-It and the I-Thou types of relationship. The scientific and technological approach has always been characterized by the former, but Buber held that the other type of relationship is also possible even with nature and that it may yield a richer harvest of understanding. Mechanical causation holds an unlimited reign in the world of It, and this is "of fundamental importance for the scientific ordering of nature."[16] But man, in his freedom, is not limited by the world of It. He can continually leave it for the I-Thou relation. Indeed, although his characteristic attitude to a tree will be that of I-It, he may yet move into an I-Thou relation with it, a mutual relation of responsiveness, aware that there is a depth there which the scientific attitude cannot disclose.[17]

Karl Heim[18] has echoed this thought in his own apologetic work, contending that science with its "It" attitude deals with what is already become, the immediate past and not the present "now." The present is a moment of responsive relationship and free decision in which man deals with a fluid and responsive nature. Once decided, present reality falls into the pattern of the "already-be-come" and appears in the causal relationships of the "It world." Heim points to the fact that energy and life alike belong, along with the essential self-transcendent I, to the nonobjectifiable realm of the dynamic present. We cannot objectify them but only what they do.[19] His whole argument again points to a psychic aspect of nature, even at the physical level, akin to will and spirit. The present is "the space of the non-objectifiable, of those possibilities, potencies, powers, volitions, which have not yet become actual."[20]

This book is no attempt to elaborate a metaphysic. It will suffice for our purpose to indicate that some of the truths in critical idealism and panpsychism are once more being recognized. It suffices here to suggest that theologically we need not be ashamed of treating nature as an interrelated whole, in which the parts are responsively related to one another and to man himself. There is an I-Thou relationship to nature which we ignore at our peril. We have an ethical responsibility to the natural order.

THE CREATIVE IMMANENCE OF GOD IN AN UNFINISHED UNIVERSE

We are left with a significant issue. If the world-process prefigures the perfect humanity of Jesus, and if the whole nexus of energy at its various levels be bound together by differing degrees of sensitivity, the directiveness of the whole towards the Christ is only intelligible if God be immanently and creatively present in the process. We have spoken of the Word as the expression of the divine intention, the depth of divine love coming forth creatively to confer being on his creatures. We have also suggested that such divine self-giving and self-emptying lies behind the whole process and is brought to a focus in the Incarnation. Such a creative expression of love becomes operative continuously within the process and directs it. This divine immanence and activity is what the biblical witnesses understand by the term Holy Spirit. We have too often confined this mode of the divine being to the ongoing and immanent presence of the Christ in the believer. But if he were prefigured beforehand in the whole process and if in him that process is being brought to its ultimate redemption, we have no justification for such a narrow limitation. When the first story of Genesis speaks of the spirit of God brooding over the abysmal deep, is there not in this the insight that the spirit of God signifies the divine activity as God is creatively immanent within his creaturely order?

We may, then, think of God as operating within the world-process and guiding it, as Hartshorne suggests, by the persuasion of love. If it is the operation of divine love, it must mean that God accepts the quasi independence of his creatures, guiding the actualization of those potencies and powers which he has given to them. The regularities of nature are an indication of the guiding rails which he sets, but when modern science speaks of scientific laws as statistical averages, this may be a reminder that ours is no deterministic universe, even at the subhuman level. Indeed, the fact that man can operate within, initiate activity, control, and, to some measure, direct nature is a reminder that nature is no closed deterministic system. We are not dealing with a mechanistic "block universe." At the present moment, as we have suggested, it is open, open to man, open to its own potencies and powers, open to God. The "block universe" is a useful scientific abstraction, and its application is to what has already become, to what Whitehead describes as actual entities which have attained satisfaction and objective immortality. This might suggest that the freedom of man must be matched by a degree of contingency in nature. Might we say that God has so made the world that he has left an area within which man may exercise that creativity which has been conferred upon him?

There are other indications in modern science that there is such an area of randomness and contingency. Our models for atomic phenomena would seem to point to an acausal structure, an element of indeterminacy in the basic stuff of the universe at the inorganic level. The most acceptable model for evolution speaks of random mutations. Rigid causal determinism is lapsing into the background as our models change. Yet the regularities described in scientific law remain to remind us that nature's powers and potencies express themselves within definite limits.

It is here that we must understand the degree of imbalance which we find in our eco-systems. It is here, too, that we may trace some of the roots of what we call natural evil—the warring systems of nature, the internecine warfare of the species, the wastage of nature in its fertility, especially at the lower levels of living things. Yet all is not evil, however much it may appear so to our humane understanding. In the evolutionary process, such factors have played their part in the creative emergence of new species and thus have made possible the ultimate emergence of man with his freedom and creativity. Furthermore, at the ecological level, they have played significant roles in the balance of nature and thus contributed to the perpetuation of life at higher levels. There is a strange cooperativeness in nature, as we have already pointed out. All is not waste and warfare, and even this sometimes serves the balance and cooperation. Once more it would seem as if nature is shot through with a network of sensitivity and creative response, as well as tragedy and suffering.

Within such a process we must see the activity of that "transcendent presence" who has also, as Creator Spirit, poured himself into his created order. He thus guides it to the fulfillment of his purpose. Yet he does so respecting that degree of independence which he has given to it and, above all, the freedom and creativity of man. That this involves him in suffering is part of his divine choice to work by the persuasion of love. This is why the present writer has spoken elsewhere of the "kenosis of Spirit."[21]

In the light of this, and including man with his freedom and creativity, we must see the universe as unfinished and open toward the future within the limits, natural and moral, which are set by the Creator. Such limits are significant at the ecological level, for two of them are the balance of the eco-systems and the moral responsibility of man. With the emergence of man and the arrival in the process of self-consciousness, God has placed the direction of that process partially under human control. This is only one aspect of that divine self-emptying which is disclosed in Jesus Christ. It is implied in Bonhoeffer's striking statement that man is coming of age[22] and in his declaration that "God would have us know that we must live as men who manage our lives without him . . . God lets himself be pushed out of the world onto the cross." One has the impression that this statement is extreme and overexaggerated. The truth in it is that God's power is the power of love and that his omnipotence is seen in the suffering and restraint of the Cross. He will not force himself on men. Rather he stands back and adopts the role of the Servant, in suffering and redemptive love. Kierkegaard saw this and wrote: "All finite power makes dependent, only omnipotence can make independent, can bring forth from nothing that which has continuance in itself by reason of the fact that omnipotence withdraws."[23] Furthermore, the Cross cannot be separated from the Resurrection with its promise of ultimate triumph. In this sense the theologians of hope point the way—God is also the power of the future. An unfinished universe will one day be finished and perfected. Its present "open-endedness" must not be taken to mean an arbitrary and contingent future. Whatever way it goes, the strategy of divine love will bring it to its appointed goal, for God is always its absolute future. Once more the key is the incarnate Christ in his risen humanity.

It is not just nature that is unfinished. Man has not fulfilled the divine image. His freedom and creativity have become misdirected by egotism and a lust for power, by laziness and indifference (what Harvey Cox describes as "leaving it to the snake").[24] He has been given powers to be fertile and people the earth and to control and subdue the subhuman realm of nature. Across the travail of the centuries he has gained scientific knowledge and technological skills which should have enabled him to develop these powers and use them aright. All his knowledge, even his science, is a divine gift. It has been pointed out that the great advances in scientific understanding occur through intuitive hunches which have the quality of disclosure.[25] For intuition and revelation come close together. Augustine had his own way of describing this, centuries ago. For him all knowledge, *scientia,* comes by divine illumination. But he also saw the tragedy of man, for man does not acknowledge the God who grants to him such ordered knowledge of his world. Man lacks *sapientia,* the wisdom that comes in Christ, and without such insight his *scientia* is misdirected. It is man's glory that he is made in God's image, capable of living and working in cooperation with God, given freedom and creativity. It is man's tragedy that he mishandles his potentiality, refuses to acknowledge the source of his powers and misdirects his knowledge.

So, with all his scientific knowledge and technological skill, man does not cooperate with the ecological balance of nature. Rather he rapes nature, upsets its balance, exploits it for his own selfish ends. He who comes out of the natural process and yet transcends it as self-conscious spirit, becomes divorced from nature because he is divorced from God. Nature, too, becomes subject to frustration. Suffering and tragedy are written across its face. Paul's magnificent dream, in which he tries to penetrate this mystery, connects the curse of nature with the curse of man. Paul Tillich can describe it as an echo of man's dream of a Golden Age when peace and harmony existed in nature and between nature and man. He adds: "It is a dream, but it contains a profound truth: man and nature belong together in their created glory, in their tragedy, and in their salvation."[26] When man violates the divinely set regularities and destroys nature's harmony, nature itself is split asunder. Only as man becomes truly man can nature also find its fulfillment. The two belong together.

The biblical witness portrays this symbolically in the story of the Garden. What could have been a garden becomes a wilderness. Man who could live in fellowship with God finds himself in a desert of his own making. Tillich in a significant sentence comments on the symbolism of the serpent: "As nature, represented by the 'Serpent,' leads man into temptation, so man, by his trespassing of the divine law, leads nature into tragedy."[27] It is almost as if the biblical witnesses are suggesting that it is nature which leads man to rebel against God and so paradoxically to mishandle nature itself. Man has been granted by and under God the capacities to produce offspring and to subdue the earth. Nature has tempted him to use these gifts apart from God, to usurp the place of his Creator and make himself lord of creation. This may be the element of truth in Wellhausen's suggestion that the tree of the knowledge of good and evil stands for civilization, but let us add the qualification that it is culture apart from God!

Professor George Williams[28] has done us all a service in pointing to the ambiguities involved in the wilderness theme in both bib-

lical thought and Western history. The great American dream of
moving out and conquering the wilderness has strangely turned
back upon us. For it is in the wilderness that nature still maintains
its balance and that the creatures in which God rejoiced at creation
can still survive and roam free. Maybe this is nearer the garden of
the story, for there man was pictured as living with God. Our
tragedy is that we have gone into the wilderness and literally made
it a desert, for we have advanced into the humanly uninhabited,
with little moral concern for nature under God. Williams points
out that, only as we are surrounded by the circumambient wilderness with its riches, "can man tend the garden in which through
the discipline and the grace of the arts and the sciences and *his
faith* [italics mine] he maintains his hold upon that life which God
created and called good."[29] Here wilderness has been reversed in
meaning, as is often evidenced in our own history. But the truth of
the garden story remains. Under God the wilderness can become a
garden. Without ethical concern it can become a true desert. Williams himself gives the word this kind of double meaning when he
remarks that, in this technological age, "the only wilderness that
will be left is what we determine shall remain untouched and that
other wilderness in the heart of man that only God can touch."[30]

But God has touched it! At one point in human history, in the
Incarnation, true humanity stands unveiled. Man has failed all
through his long history to fulfill his potentials and attain his true
nature in God's image, and, in so doing, he has failed to fulfill nature itself. But in the Christ, man and nature alike are manifested
in the wholeness that God intended, and in Christ the dark estrangement in both nature and man is overcome. The Christ comes to
crown the process, but also to redeem it in its totality, even though
that redemption still in part be promise. The forces of estrangement,
separation, tragedy in the universe are overcome in him. ". . . there
is no salvation of man if there is no salvation of nature, for man is
in nature and nature is in man."[31]

Co-workers with God and Ethical Responsibility

There is a specifically humanist stance over this issue of ecology
and what might be called an ethical responsibility which has secular

roots. Indeed, over this matter as over so many other contemporary problems such as race and poverty, initiative has often been taken by the secularist and the humanist while the Church has lagged behind. Nor would this writer dispute that God is using such activity. From the Christian standpoint we have too long refused to see God in many places where genuine concern is being manifested and have limited the divine presence to the confines of an avowedly Christian commitment. We have forgotten the parabolic picture of Jesus that to give a cup of cold water, to relieve poverty, to visit the imprisoned, to show concern for others may also be serving him. We have also glossed over the words in the prologue of the Gospel of John, in which the Word is declared to be the light that enlightens all men. May we say that wherever men see light, meaning, and act in accordance with it, they may be serving the Christ, even though they do not acknowledge him? If I adopt a Christian stance, I have no right to condemn my fellow who shows a like concern but from a different motivation. This does not mean, of course, that I may not see a deeper motivation than that of which he is aware.

However, we are here concerned with the Christian attitude to the environmental problem. This means that we have to remind ourselves about the nature of the Christian. Bonhoeffer once defined a Christian as one in whom the Christ is forming his form again.[32] The new man, the true humanity, man before God and truly in his image, has been actualized in the Incarnation. But it does not end there, for we have to do with a risen Christ who is still God-man in the glory of his risen humanity. Into that humanity the believer is incorporated. In the commitment of faith, he too passes through the pattern of death and resurrection and thereby becomes conformed to the image of Christ. A Christian is not one who struggles to become or who imitates Christ. He is one in whom the form of Christ takes form, and this is the work of the Christ himself. The Christian is drawn into the form of Jesus Christ and participates in his risen humanity. He is redeemed. Christ sets him free to be the kind of man that God intended. What he is potentially as God created him, he becomes as he is drawn into the humanity of the Incarnate and Risen Christ.

Now the form of Christ is that of the Incarnate God-man. So

for a man to be transformed into His image, to be formed in His likeness, implies that the Christ gives to him and empowers him to manifest those qualities and capacities which are present in the Incarnation. But if man so participates in the Incarnation, then he should be showing, however imperfectly, the marks of that Incarnation. Foremost among these will be the capacity for self-emptying, for outgoing love, for redemptive concern, which marks his Lord. The love of Christ flows into those who are re-created in his form and so out to their fellows. It also moves back to God in whose outpouring they themselves have been both created and redeemed. It is this love and concern which provides the central motivation for a Christian ethic. Now such love and concern, if it expresses the conformation to the image of Christ, should be directed on nature as well as on man. Our Lord Himself showed a reverence for all creation, drew from its life for his parables, saw it as the object of the Father's love. Paul saw all creation suffering with man. This description stands as a paradigm of the Christian man.

At this point the environmental issue lifts its head. What does such a motivation imply with regard to nature? We Christians have been very vocal about our responsibility to our fellow humans, but have we no responsibility to nature? We have already discussed at length the Hebrew understanding of man's covenant relation with nature, broken though it may be. A man should respect the life of his beast. He should recognize that nature has a life of its own, leaving his ground fallow periodically, leaving corners of his field of grain unreaped. This suggests at once that we might expect of the Christian a reverence and respect for nature, a regard for its processes, a concern for its life.

Albert Schweitzer is a controversial figure. Was he theist or pantheist, Christian or humanist? He was perhaps not a Christian in the orthodox sense, but who can deny that in his sacrificial service and in his concern for suffering humanity, he showed that he was being conformed to the form of the Christ? Who, too, can escape that haunting paragraph at the end of *The Quest:* "He comes to us as One unknown, without a name, as of old, by the lakeside, He came to those men who knew Him not. He speaks to us the same word: 'Follow thou me!' and sets us to the tasks which He has to fulfil for our time. He commands. And to those who obey Him, whether they be wise or simple, He will reveal Himself in the toils, the conflicts, the sufferings which they shall pass through in His fellowship, and, as an ineffable mystery, they shall learn in their own experience Who He is."[33] It is not surprising that he should make the main premise of his ethical stance, a "reverence for life." For this is one of the qualities displayed by our Lord himself who manifested a reverence for nature and a love for natural things throughout his teaching. It is true that this "reverence for life" verges often in Schweitzer into a kind of mystical pantheism, but he did show us an attitude towards nature which orthodox Christianity has strangely lacked.

Schweitzer notes sadly the tendency of Western and Oriental philosophers alike to limit ethical concern to the human level. For him all things are activated by a will to live, and thus there must be a reverence for even cells and crystals.[34] He was, however, disturbed by the dilemma that nature presented—the necessity to destroy life. He recognized that natural things did in this way subserve the ecological balance, and he wrote: "Again and again we see ourselves under the necessity of saving one living creature by destroying or damaging another."[35] In his autobiography he rejoices that sleeping sickness has been cured but sadly reflects that to save life in this way the disease-causing germs have to be killed. He regrets that to preserve the life of a young fish-eagle, numberless small fishes have to be killed.[36] He thus has to face the problem of the ecological pyramid, but he does counsel an ethical attitude toward it, a reverence for it that yet prevents its excesses: "So far as he is a free man he (man) uses every opportunity of tasting the blessedness of being able to assist life and avert from it suffering and destruction."[37] But what is this but aiding in the redemption of nature from its vanity and frustration! Schweitzer's final comment on traditional Christianity is significant: "Even when sympathy with the animal creation was felt to be right, it could not be brought within the scope of ethics, because ethics were really focused only on the behavior of man to man."[38]

If we leave on one side the near-pantheism of Schweitzer with his emphasis on the Will-to-Live immanent in all things, he is yet pointing to a vital lack in the Christian understanding of ethical responsibility. What he says about reverence for life becomes more significant if we see nature itself as capable of and knit together by sensitivity and psychic response. What Buber refers to as an I-Thou relationship with nature involves an acceptance of the creatures for what they are, a reverence for their particular type of being, a concern for their freedom from suffering and frustration within the limits that ecological balance permits, a recognition of their kinship with us. For we who transcend nature as self-conscious spirits are yet also one with nature from which we have emerged by God's creative act. We need to recognize our oneness with nature and to seek to grasp its spiritual meaning.

Paul Tillich has suggested that in art, painters and sculptors can creatively transform nature and make it bear spiritual meaning. He describes this as "nature elevated above itself, revealing its tragedy and, at the same time, its victory over its tragedy."[39] But there is a much more significant and practical aspect of our recognition of kinship with all creatures. This is to use our scientific knowledge and technological skills so that we respect nature's balance, seeking to remove its imbalance and to remedy its tragedy and suffering. In this sense we become co-workers with God in the redemption of nature. Just as we cannot be finally saved without nature, so as those in whom the form of Christ is being formed, we must cooperate with our Lord in his redemptive mission. In us the Incarnation is extended in history as we are drawn into the risen humanity of the Christ. Because of this, our task is to heal the hurt of nature, redeem it from its frustration and transience, and direct it to higher and spiritual ends while respecting its independence. We are to set it free that it may not serve our selfish economic ends and be subject to our arrogant exploitation. It longs to be drawn into the Christ that it may serve the ends of his Kingdom; for it too is waiting with longing for the unveiling of the sons of God, the new humanity in Christ.

We need the spirit of St. Francis of Assisi who in the great "Canticle of the Sun" could recognize his kinship with all living things.[40] So he could sing of brother son and sister moon, of brother wind and sister water, of brother fire and mother earth, praising his and their Creator for the role they played in his own life. The canticle is full of rejoicing and wonder at these creatures which play their allotted part in the divine economy. But we have lost this sense of joy and wonder in our experience of nature. A naturalistic thinker like Julian Huxley can write: "Enjoyment as well as material resources are being threatened (by our rape of nature); as my brother Aldous said after reading Rachel Carson's book (*Silent Spring*), we are exterminating half the basis of English poetry!" [parentheses mine][41] Our scientific atmosphere has nullified the desire to rejoice and celebrate and reduced nature and all its constituent creatures to "Its." We do not see them as "Thous" but as objects which science and technology can use and control. They have become means to our economic ends rather than ends in themselves. We have forgotten that our God rejoiced in his creation and declared it to be good because it contained potentially all the possibilities for the realization of his purpose.

Here is our deepest motivation for an ethical concern at this level. For in and through nature, the Christian meets his Creator. His "Thou" relation with nature merges into a "Thou" relation to that personal Presence who journeys with his creatures and sustains their life. The whole universe can be sacramental in the sense that it mediates the presence of and points to its Creator. In the sacraments of the church this sacramental aspect of nature is brought to a focus. For we take bread and wine and water, elements symbolic of all nature, and make them the bearers of spiritual meaning. Nature participates in the process of salvation. It becomes united to God. The creatures of the old creation are elevated into creatures of the new creation. So nature attains its true and ultimate meaning. Bonhoeffer suggests that in the sacraments the creatures "are freed from their dumbness and proclaim directly to the believer the new creative Word of God. They no longer need man's interpretation. Enslaved nature does not utter the Word of creation directly to us. But the sacraments speak."[42] They are drawn up into Christ's risen humanity and prefigure that ultimate consummation when men and nature alike shall be gathered up in Christ. So in worship and in action, we in whom the Christ is pleased to create a new humanity become co-workers with him in the redemption of all things.

One other significant aspect of all this lies at the level of human relationships—the relation of the population burst to the environmental issue. Christians need to take a new look at the issue of sex relationships and the procreation of children. They were made to produce and inhabit the earth, but to do so responsibly under God. I find it difficult to understand the conservative and limited attitude of some Christians to this, including the Catholic hierarchy. It would seem that the proper use of contraceptives and responsible family planning are necessary in the Christian's responsibility to his world, and not only for the Christian but also for all men. The Christian view of sex has too long been tied to a perverted view of original sin. We need to see it as God's gift and a natural sacrament, in which procreation is only one aspect and in which the deep and abiding communion of two human beings is also a significant dimension. We are psychosomatic wholes, and the true expression of the I-Thou relation, at its most intimate level of marriage, has its somatic and natural dimensions as well as its spiritual. Even the new humanity in Christ does not leave sex behind so long as it is lived in the form of this world.

THE INCARNATION AND A COSMIC HOPE

We can be grateful that contemporary theology has recovered a concern with the future and a futuristic eschatology. As we have already indicated, this often becomes so dominant that it almost confines God to the future and majors on a temporal model of divine transcendence, with God as the absolute future. God is the overarching reality, the all-embracing ground, the transcendent presence who accompanies his creatures throughout their pilgrimage. We have sought to think of him as the transcendent personal depth in this process who is immanently present and active within it. We have pictured him, in his triunity, as coming forth out of his depth of love in creative and redemptive activity as Word/Son and operating immanently within his creation as Spirit. We have seen the whole process as one which both enriches his life by its actuality and yet is borne by him in suffering and redemptive love. We have stressed the Incarnation as the focal point in which the creative process reaches its climax in the full and true humanity of Jesus.

Here God brings his redemptive suffering to its climax and crowns his creation in the God-man. God creates a new humanity and promises a new heaven and a new earth in the risen humanity of the Christ. The Resurrection becomes the key to the future and declares that our labor as co-workers with God shall not be cast like rubbish on the void. We live in hope as well as in faith and love.

It is in this sense that we can describe the Christ as the "incarnate eschaton," for here the future has become present in one historical life. If he is the climax of the process, if in him the divine meaning of the process is made plain, then his Resurrection and his risen humanity are the promise of that ultimate destiny to which the whole process is directed. God is bringing the whole creation to that point when, as Paul saw, all things shall be united, summed up, in Christ, things in heaven and things on earth (Eph. 1:10). The recurring theme that all things shall be put in subjection under Christ and God shall be all in all points likewise to a cosmic eschatology (1 Cor. 15:27, 28; Phil. 3:21; cf. Heb. 2:8, 9). So also does the vision of a new heaven and a new earth (Rev. 21:1). In other words, the Christian hope points to a resurrection, a creative renewal of the whole process.

We note the centrality of the Incarnation. All things are to be summed up in the Christ, gathered into his new creation, of which his risen humanity is the nucleus. Pittenger's insight is so true to the biblical witness—God is incarnating himself in his creation. What was begun in Jesus of Nazareth will be completed in the final consummation. The final unveiling of the sons of God—the new humanity begun in the Incarnation, hidden in the Christian believer and the Church within the movement of the process—will bring with it the final redemption and transformation of nature too. Teilhard's description of the new stage of evolution as a movement towards the hyperpersonal in which Christification is taking place fails at just this point. As we have seen, it is highly problematical whether he includes the natural order along with humanity.

Karl Heim, to whom we have already referred and whose eclipse in the fifties is now being remedied, greatly emphasized this cosmic eschatology and the promise of the Resurrection of the Christ.[43] As he points out, human reason cannot dictate the final activity of a free and loving God. The biblical imagery and its theological expressions appear to the rational mind and the scientific attitude as pure mythology. Yet science, too, has its myths—the models it builds for the explosive beginning and the "heat-death" end of the universe. Faith simply paints a bigger and redemptive canvas. The pessimism of the rigid application of the Second Law of Thermodynamics is, at best, but an extrapolation to the whole universe of our limited experience of what happens in a finite and closed system of nature. We cannot dogmatically affirm that the infinite universe is itself a closed system—this is a matter of speculative faith. But if we are dealing with the God of Jesus Christ, we move to a different level and use language that is also full of models and symbols, analogies and myths. All we can affirm is what the Resurrection promises. We do not know how the cosmos shall be transformed and given a spiritual significance. We do not know how its present clothing of transience and decay, vanity and frustration, shall be shed. But we see Jesus, and we believe that God who lifted this life into his own is the power of the future. His all-embracing, creative, and redeeming love will gather us all in. We do not know what such a redeemed cosmos will be like, for in our science we have to do with it in its clothing of corruption and frustration. As Heim says: ". . . we are utterly dependent on His almighty power for the answer to the question as to the method of the change."[44]

Now, as Moltmann has so ably put it, we do not sit down and wait for the consummation. In a way that he would not accept, we can declare that the Kingdom is already with us, forming itself within the form of this world. Like a chrysalis, this world carries within itself the absolute future. The Christ in his risen humanity is present in its midst fulfilling his task, and we are his co-workers. What we do in the mission of redeeming our fellows, redeeming society, and redeeming our natural environment plays its part in the final outcome. This world is unfinished, but we also are serving with and in the Christ in moving it to its final consummation. How and when that End comes depends in part upon the role that Christians, yes and others too, play in the setting free of men, society and nature alike. For God through Christ has put into the hands of men the capacity to set free the potencies and powers which, in the beginning of the creative process, were implanted by God and which carry with them possibilities that only his future will unveil. It is to the setting free of such possibilities in man and nature alike that he calls us in the Christ. This is what Moltmann calls "creative discipleship." The Resurrection has made possible the extension of the Incarnation in the lives of men and the life of the world. That process of "Christification" continues as, in creative discipleship, we become the servants of the world in and through whom the Christ is pleased to work. In such a setting, eschatological hope and ethical responsibility both have their significant place.

EPILOGUE

Christian Ecotactics

WHAT CAN THE CHRISTIAN DO APART FROM THE ecological concern of secular men, humanists and naturalists? Let us, as before, affirm our oneness with them in common concern and in the task of cleaning mankind's spaceship. There is no need here to go into the detailed ecotactics which are stated in such excellent volumes as *The Environmental Handbook* and *Ecotactics*. Our concern is rather with anything distinctive in the Christian approach and also in the Christian contribution to the environmental enterprise.

First of all, we need to remember the distinctive Christian motivation. As with all dimensions of Christian ethics, it is rooted in the disclosure of God in Jesus Christ and in the testimony of the biblical witnesses. Grounded in God's love for men and for his world, it shows a concern for nature based on that which God showed in his creative act for the creation as a whole and which Jesus the Christ manifested in his earthly ministry. We are concerned for nature because it, too, is God's creation. Furthermore, we are concerned for nature in hope because it is a participant in the redemption that the Christ has effected in his incarnate life, death, and resurrection.

138

So we strive to remove the frustration of nature and prepare the way for God's final coming. And subsidiary to this, we are concerned for nature because we men have failed in our responsibility to it as sharing with us in God's creative act. We must, under God, right the wrong that men have done, restore the balance of nature, and as Christ's servants aid in its redemption. We must make clear that the groaning and travailing of nature is now in part being healed as the redemption of men, too, moves to its final consummation and as the sons of God are being unveiled. We act with faith in God, love to our fellow men and our natural environment, hope in the final summing up of all things in the Christ. Our ethical concern has thus a deeper dimension.

Secondly, the Church needs to emphasize both this Christian motivation and its theological roots in its preaching and teaching. If the Church is truly to exercise its mission as the servant community, it will need to list among the urgent needs of men, not only the basic issues of personal and social redemption, but also their relation to and mishandling of their environment. If redemption means the end of alienation and estrangement and the discovery of the meaning of life as lived within the divine purpose, such a life has environmental as well as social dimensions. It is not much use being concerned with social injustice and economic inequity if we show no concern for the natural setting without which life in every aspect would be impossible. If our environment goes dead, then all our social concern will be of little avail, and we might as well concentrate on getting people out of hell into heaven. But, as we have seen, this is not anywhere near the full eschatological dimension of the gospel.

We need to organize church conferences in which the ecological issues are discussed, in which the biblical view of nature is made clear, in which the theological dimension of the environmental problem is considered, and in which the ethical dimension of our relation to nature is stressed. There can be no effective action without adequate understanding. This can be offered in preaching and occasional lectures, but it will be most effective in dialogue. Many excellent films and books are available at the secular level and are listed in the two books mentioned at the beginning of this Epilogue. The

Church should be the conscience of the community. The Church has failed only too sadly here. It has not been the communal conscience on many of the social and racial issues of our day. Rather it has let humanists and even politicians get in before it. Perhaps we can exercise our Christian responsibility better when it applies to our natural environment! But to do this we shall have to be informed.

Thirdly, Christians need to activate groups of people to translate Christian concern into action. Parts of the community which have been mishandled with trash, creeks in which garbage has been carelessly dumped, seashores where special emergencies arise from oil seepage and bird life is endangered—one could give a long list of projects, some arising out of immediate emergencies and some which deal with long-standing ecological problems. Student groups and groups of concerned citizens have often pointed the way here, and the Christian communities have often participated, individually and as church groups. It would be great if the church here gave a lead. So often it is accused by secular man of dragging its feet and concentrating on the other-worldly. Here is an opportunity to demonstrate our this-worldly concern at a new level and to convince our fellows that the Christian faith is world-affirming.

Fourthly, Christians should be encouraged to join conservation groups, to exert pressures on governmental bodies at all levels, and to voice strong opposition when evident industrial greed and the profit motive are behind efforts which will increase environmental pollution or destroy some natural setting and its wild life. Lawyers with Christian convictions need to devise ways to prevent big corporations from "getting by" with so much environmental pollution. Politicans and legislators with Christian convictions need to be encouraged to attack this issue as zealously as their humanistic and secular colleagues. Christian convictions should mean a personal integrity that can withstand the lobbying tactics of industrial interests and the pressure of political expediency. Such men should have the support of the churches, irrespective of their political labels. By this I mean that the Church need not be accused of "going political," if it makes it clear to its members that the ecological issue is one on which all men of good will, irrespective of political party, should be united. In addition, letters to legislators and public officials should be encouraged when a particular and vital matter relating to the natural environment is under consideration.

Finally, the Christian is the conscience of society, the leaven in the lump. The anonymous author of *Ad Diognetum* could declare early in the second century A.D. that what the soul is to the body, the Christian is to the world. Let us close with a telling quotation from C. A. Coulson, himself a distinguished scientist: "Only those who know the inner nature of Man, and the peculiar ways in which God transforms man's mind by the renewing power of His Spirit, and the status which God confers upon him that he may be called a child of God, are big enough to speak to the condition of today."[1]

NOTES

PROLOGUE

1. T. E. Jessop, *Science and the Spiritual* (London: Christian News Letter Books, The Sheldon Press, 1942), p. 63.

CHAPTER I

1. Gerhard Von Rad, *Old Testament Theology* (New York: Harper & Row, 1966), 1:48–56.
2. Rudolf Bultmann, *Theology of the New Testament* (New York: Charles Scribner's Sons, 1951), 1:30.

CHAPTER II

1. Marston Bates, "Ecology and Evolution," *Evolution after Darwin: Vol. 1 The Evolution of Life,* ed. Sol Tax (Chicago: Chicago University Press, 1960), p. 547.
2. Ibid.
3. Ronald A. Fisher, *The Genetical Theory of Natural Selection,* 2d ed. (New York: Dover, 1958).
4. Theodosius Dobzhansky, *Genetics and the Origin of Species,* 3d ed. (New York: Columbia University Press, 1951).
5. Cf. E. C. Rust, *Science and Faith* (New York: Oxford University Press, 1967, pp. 149 ff.
6. See Theodosius Dobzhansky, *Mankind Evolving* (New Haven: Yale University Press, 1962), p. 199.
7. Ibid.
8. Ibid.
9. Ibid., p. 203.
10. Ibid., p. 154.
11. For details, see Rust, *Science and Faith,* pp. 153 ff.
12. Marston Bates, *The Nature of Natural History* (New York: Charles Scribner's Sons, 1950), p. 235.

13. Theodosius Dobzhansky, "Evolution and Environment," *The Evolution of Life,* ed. Tax, p. 405.

14. Bates, "Ecology and Evolution," p. 213.

15. Peter Kroptkin, *Mutual Aid* (London: Penguin Books, 1939).

16. L. Richmond Wheeler, source of quotation not traced but contained in a book in University of Leeds Brotherton Library, England.

17. This is discussed at length in *Science and Faith,* pp. 157 ff.

18. See Michael Polanyi, *Personal Knowledge* (Chicago: University of Chicago Press, 1958), pp. 384 ff.

19. Dobzhansky, "Evolution and Environment," p. 425.

20. Cf. A. Whofsky, "A Hundred Years of Darwinism in Biology," *Darwin's Vision and Christian Perspectives,* ed. W. J. Ong (New York: Macmillan, 1960), p. 29.

21. L. J. Henderson, *The Fitness of the Environment* (Boston: Beacon Press, 1958), p. 255.

22. Ibid., p. 272.

23. Ibid., p. 279.

24. Bates, *The Nature of Natural History,* p. 122.

25. Ibid., p. 124.

26. Ibid., pp. 131 ff.

27. Ibid., pp. 112 ff.

28. Alfred M. Elliott, *Zoology* (New York: Appleton-Century-Crofts, 1963), p. 132.

CHAPTER III

1. Theodosius Dobzhansky, *Mankind Evolving* (New Haven: Yale University Press, 1963), p. 337.

2. A. I. Hellowell, "Culture, Personality, and Society," *Anthropology Today,* ed. Alfred L. Kroeber (Chicago: University of Chicago Press, 1953), p. 620, quoted in Dobzhansky,. *Mankind Evolving,* p. 338.

3. W. H. Thorpe, *Biology and the Nature of Man* (London: Oxford University Press, 1962), p. 59.

4. Michael Polanyi, *Personal Knowledge* (Chicago: University of Chicago Press, 1958), *passim;* and Michael Polanyi, *The Tacit Dimension* (Garden City: Doubleday Anchor Books, 1967), *passim.*

5. Polanyi, *Personal Knowledge,* p. 267.

6. Cf. ibid.

7. Ibid., p. 299.

8. See T. H. Huxley and Julian Huxley, *Evolution and Ethics,*

1893-1943 (London: Pilot Press Ltd., 1947, and New York: Kraus Reprint Co., 1969); also C. H. Waddington, *The Ethical Animal* (Chicago: University of Chicago Press, 1967).

9. Thorpe, *Biology and the Nature of Man,* p. 91.

10. G. L. Stebbins, "Prospects for Spaceship Man," *Saturday Review,* 7 March 1970, p. 50.

11. Cited in C. A. Coulson, *Science, Technology and the Christian* (New York: Abingdon Press, 1960), p. 39.

12. Quoted in ibid., pp. 37 ff.

13. Referred to in Jacob Bronowski, *Science and Human Values* (New York: Harper & Bros., 1959), p. 91.

14. Consult Frank Graham, Jr., *Since Silent Spring* (Boston: Houghton Mifflin Co., 1970).

15. R. & L. Rienow, *Moment in the Sun* (New York: Ballantine Books, 1969), p. 128.

16. Ibid., p. 129.

17. Cf. ibid., pp. 94 ff. and 220 ff.

18. For details, consult Wesley Marx, *The Frail Ocean* (New York: Ballantine Books, 1967), pp. 61 ff.

19. Consult especially Rachel Carson, *Silent Spring* (Greenwich: Fawcett Publications, 1970), and Graham, *Since Silent Spring.*

20. Marx, pp. 63 ff.

21. Ibid., pp. 64 ff.

22. Paul R. Ehrlich, "Eco-Catastrophe," *The Environmental Handbook,* ed. Garrett de Bell (New York: Ballantine Books, 1970), pp. 161 ff.

23. Marx, pp. 12–23.

24. For details, consult Rienow, pp. 141 ff.

25. Consult Paul R. Ehrlich, *The Population Bomb* (New York: Ballantine Books, 1968).

26. Ibid., pp. 69 ff. and 158 ff.

27. Hal Borland, review of *Since Silent Spring,* by Graham, in *Saturday Review,* 4 April 1970, p. 59.

28. Consult Robert E. Cook, William Haseltine, and Arthur W. Galston, "What Have We Done to Vietnam?" *The New Republic,* 10 January 1970, pp. 18–21.

29. Ridgeway, "You Don't Need a Sewerman," *Motive,* April/May 1970, pp. 77 ff.

30. Ibid., p. 80.

31. Consult Norman Cousins, "New York's Fight against Pollution," *Saturday Review*, 7 March 1970, pp. 53 ff.

32. Ibid., p. 55.

33. For details, see *The Environmental Handbook*. pp. 312 ff.

CHAPTER IV

1. See especially Alfred North Whitehead, *Science and the Modern World* (London: Cambridge University Press, 1932); *Process and Reality* (London: Cambridge University Press, 1929); *Adventures of Ideas* (New York: Mentor Books, 1955).

2. For a more detailed treatment of Whitehead's thought, see Eric C. Rust, *Evolutionary Philosophies and Contemporary Theology* (Philadelphia: Westminster Press, 1969), pp. 98 ff.

3. Consult Paul Ostreicher, ed., *The Christian-Marxist Dialogue* (New York: Macmillan, 1969); T. W. Ogletree, ed., *Openings for Marxist Christian Dialogue* (Nashville: Abingdon Press, 1968); Roger Garaudy, *From Anathema to Dialogue* (New York: Random House, 1968); Ernst Bloch, *Man on His Own*, trans. E. B. Ashton (New York: Herder and Herder, 1970).

4. Roger Garaudy, *Karl Marx: The Evolution of His Thought* (New York: International Publishers, 1967).

5. Harvey Cox, "Foreword," in Bloch, *Man on His Own*, p. 10.

6. Ogletree, p. 30.

7. Samuel Alexander, *Space, Time and Deity*, 2 vols. (London: Macmillan, 1934). See also Rust, *Evolutionary Philosophies and Contemporary Theology*.

8. Jürgen Moltmann, "Hope without Faith: Humanism without God," *Is God Dead: Concilium* (New York: Paulist Press, 1966), 16:31.

9. Garaudy, *From Anathema to Dialogue*, p. 94.

10. Bloch, pp. 222 ff.

11. Ibid., p. 224.

12. Ibid., p. 225.

13. Garaudy, *From Anathema to Dialogue*, p. 9.

14. Bloch, p. 222.

15. Ibid., p. 239.

16. Ibid.

17. Ibid., pp. 238 ff.

18. See these books by the following authors: Norman Pittenger,

God in Process (London: SCM Press, 1967), *Process Thought and Christian Faith* (New York: Macmillan, 1968), *The Word Incarnate* (New York: Harper & Bros., 1959); Daniel Day Williams, *God's Grace and Man's Hope* (New York: Harper & Bros., 1949), *The Spirit and the Forms of Love* (New York: Harper & Row, 1968); Richard Overman, *Evolution and the Christian Doctrine of Creation* (Philadelphia: Westminster, 1967); Charles Hartshorne, *The Divine Relativity* (New Haven: Yale University Press, 1964), *Reality As a Social Process* (Boston: Beacon Press, 1953), *Man's Vision of God* (Chicago: Willett Clark & Co., 1941), *The Logic of Perfection* (LaSalle: Open Court, 1962); and John B. Cobb, Jr., *A Christian Natural Theology* (Philadelphia: Westminster, 1965).

19. Hartshorne, *The Divine Relativity,* p. 136.

20. Williams, *The Spirit and the Forms of Love,* p. 125.

21. Charles Hartshorne and William L. Reese, *Philosophers Speak of God* (Chicago: University of Chicago Press, 1953), pp. 1–15.

22. Pittenger, *Process Thought and Christian Faith,* p. 44.

23. Pittenger, *The Word Incarnate,* p. 226.

24. Pittenger, *Process Thought and Christian Faith,* p. 24.

25. Pittenger, *God in Process,* p. 17.

26. Pittenger, *Process Thought and Christian Faith,* p. 33.

27. Ibid., p. 47.

28. Pittenger, *God in Process,* p. 27. Cf. *The Word Incarnate.*

29. Pittenger, *Process Thought and Christian Faith,* p. 52.

30. Pittenger, *God in Process,* p. 93.

31. Ibid., p. 20.

32. Ibid.

33. Teilhard de Chardin, *The Phenomenon of Man,* trans. B. Wall (New York: Harper & Bros., 1959); *The Future of Man,* trans. N. Denny (New York: Harper & Row, 1964); *The Divine Milieu* (New York: Harper & Bros., 1960).

34. Teilhard de Chardin, *The Vision of the Past* (New York: Harper & Row, 1966), p. 242.

35. Teilhard, *The Future of Man,* p. 306.

36. Ibid., p. 307.

37. Ibid.

38. From a diary entry, 12 December 1919. Cited in Piet Smulders, *The Design of Teilhard de Chardin,* trans. A. Gibson (Westminster, Md.: Newman Press, 1967), p. 126.

39. Teilhard, *The Future of Man,* p. 304.

40. Cited in Emile Rideau, *The Thought of Teilhard de Chardin,* trans. R. Hague (New York: Harper & Row, 1965), pp. 522 ff.

41. Teilhard, *The Phenomenon of Man,* p. 289.

42. Teilhard, *The Future of Man,* p. 233.

43. See these books by the following authors: Jürgen Moltmann, *The Theology of Hope,* trans. J. W. Leitch (New York: Harper & Row, 1967), *Religion, Revolution, and the Future,* trans. M. D. Meeks (New York: Charles Scribner's Sons, 1969); Wolfhart Pannenberg, *Jesus: God and Man,* trans. L. L. Wilkins and D. A. Priebe (Philadelphia: Westminster, 1968), *Theology and the Kingdom of God* (Philadelphia: Westminster, 1969); Wolfhart Pannenberg, ed., *Revelation As History,* trans. D. Branskou (New York: Macmillan, 1968), *Hermeneutic and History* (New York: Harper & Row, 1967); Johannes B. Metz, *The Theology of the World,* trans. W. Glenn-Doepel (New York: Herder & Herder, 1969); Edward Schillebeeckx, *God the Future of Man,* trans. N. D. Smith (New York: Sheed & Ward, 1968).

44. Carl E. Braaten, *The Future of God* (New York: Harper & Row, 1969).

45. Pannenberg, *Jesus: God and Man,* pp. 88–106.

46. Pannenberg, *Theology and the Kingdom of God,* p. 60.

47. Cf. Pannenberg's attack on Barth in *Jesus: God and Man,* pp. 33 ff.

48. Pannenberg, *Theology and the Kingdom of God,* p. 59.

49. Cf. Karl Heim, *God Transcendent,* trans. E. P. Dickie (London: Nisbet & Co., Ltd., 1935).

50. Pannenberg, *Theology and the Kingdom of God,* p. 60.

51. Ibid., p. 66.

52. Ibid., pp. 62 ff.

53. Ibid., p. 66.

54. Ibid., p. 68.

55. Pannenberg, *Jesus: God and Man,* p. 395.

56. Ibid., p. 396.

57. Moltmann, *The Theology of Hope,* p. 333.

58. Ibid., p. 335.

59. Metz, p. 95.

60. Ibid., pp. 94 ff.

Chapter V

1. There is an excellent discussion of the thought of F. D. Maurice in Alec Vidler, *F. D. Maurice and Company* (London: SCM Press, 1966). See especially pp. 38 ff.

2. From *Life of F. D. Maurice,* 2:358, quoted in Vidler, *F. D. Maurice and Company,* p. 43.

3. F. D. Maurice, *Patriarchs and Law Givers* (London: Macmillan, 1892), p. 66.

4. Dietrich Bonhoeffer, *Letters and Papers from Prison,* trans. R. Fuller and ed. E. Bethge (New York: Macmillan, 1967), p. 213.

5. Dietrich Bonhoeffer, *Christ the Center,* trans. John Bowden (New York: Harper & Row, 1960), p. 45.

6. Ibid., p. 46.

7. Cf. Martin Buber, *I and Thou,* trans. Gregor Smith (Edinburg: T. & T. Clark, 1937).

8. Cf. Dietrich Bonhoeffer, essay in *Gesammelte Schriften* (Munich: Chr. Kaiser, n.d.), 3:103 ff.

9. Bonhoeffer, *Letters and Papers from Prison,* p. 155.

10. Ibid., p. 210.

11. I am indebted in the following paragraphs to insights of John Macquarrie, "The Pre-existence of Jesus Christ," *The Expository Times,* (1966), 77:199 ff., although I do not concur with all his thinking.

12. Ibid., p. 202.

13. Paul Tillich, *The Shaking of the Foundations* (London: SCM, 1949), p. 82.

14. T. E. Jessop, *Science and the Spritual* (London: Sheldon, 1942), p. 61.

15. Buber, *passim.*

16. Ibid., p. 51.

17. Ibid., pp. 7 ff.

18. Karl Heim, *God Transcendent,* trans. E. Dickie (London: Nesbet, 1935), pp. 103–152. Now once more being studied in Germany.

19. Ibid., pp. 132 ff.

20. Ibid., p. 136.

21. Eric C. Rust, *Science and Faith* (New York: Oxford University Press, 1967), pp. 195 ff.

22. Bonhoeffer, *Letters and Papers from Prison*, p. 196.

23. Søren Kierkegaard, *Journal*, included in a footnote in W. Lowrie, trans., *Christian Discourses* (London: Oxford University Press, 1939), p. 187. This quotation is cited in Eric C. Rust, *Towards a Theological Understanding of History* (New York: Oxford University Press, 1963), p. 145, where I have a much fuller discussion of the omnipotence of divine love.

24. Harvey Cox, *On Not Leaving It to the Snake* (New York: Macmillan, 1968).

25. Cf. Rust, *Science and Faith*, pp. 314 ff.

26. Tillich, p. 83.

27. Ibid.

28. George H. Williams, *Wilderness and Paradise in Christian Thought* (New York: Harper & Bros., 1962), pp. 1–137.

29. Ibid., p. 137.

30. Ibid., p. 136.

31. Tillich, p. 84.

32. Dietrich Bonhoeffer, *Ethics*, trans. N. H. Smith (New York: Macmillan, 1955), pp. 17 ff.

33. Albert Schweitzer, *The Quest of the Historical Jesus*, trans. W. Montgomery (London: A. & C. Black, 1945), p. 401.

34. See Albert Schweitzer, *Civilization and Ethics*, trans. C. T. Campion (London: A. & C. Black, 1946), p. 213.

35. Albert Schweitzer, *Indian Thought and Its Development*, trans. Mrs. Charles E. Russell (Magnolia, Mass.: Peter Smith, 1962), p. 84.

36. Albert Schweitzer, *Out of My Life and Thought* (London: George Allen & Unwin, 1933), pp. 271 ff.

37. Ibid., p. 272.

38. Ibid.

39. Tillich, p. 85.

40. For the original text and Matthew Arnold's translation, consult A. Sabatier, *Life of St. Francis of Assisi* (London: Hodder and Stoughton, 1900), pp. 304 ff.

41. Julius Huxley, "The Future of Man—Evolutionary Aspects," *Man and His Future*, ed. Gordon Wolstenholme (Boston: Little, Brown, 1963), p. 10.

42. Bonhoeffer, *Christ the Center*, p. 67; cf. Tillich, p. 86.

43. Karl Heim, *The World: Its Creation and Consummation,* trans. Robert Smith (Philadelphia: Muhlenberg Press, 1962), pp. 101–150.
44. Ibid., p. 148.

EPILOGUE

1. C. A. Coulson, *Science, Technology and the Christian* (Nashville: Abingdon, 1960), p. 109.